LOVE SONG OF THE DARK LORD

Jayadeva's *Gītagovinda*

Prepared for the Columbia College Program of
Translations from the Oriental Classics

New York
Columbia University Press

EDITED AN

Love Song of the Dark Lord

Jayadeva's *Gītagovinda*

TRANSLATED BY BARBARA STOLER MILLER

UNESCO COLLECTION OF REPRESENTATIVE WORKS

INDIAN SERIES

This book
has been accepted
in the Indian Series
of the Translations Collection
of the United Nations
Educational, Scientific and Cultural Organization
(UNESCO)

———•◆———

Columbia University Press
New York   Guildford, Surrey
Printed in the United States of America
LIBRARY OF CONGRESS CATALOGING IN PUBLICATION DATA
Jayadeva, son of Bhojadeva.
Love Song of the Dark Lord, Jayadeva's Gītagovinda
"Translations from the Oriental classics."
1. Krishna—Poetry. I. Miller, Barbara Stoler. II. Title.
PK3794.J3G53 1977   891'.2'1   76-13168
ISBN 0-231-04029-6 pbk.
p 10 9 8 7
c 10 9 8 7 6 5 4 3

To Tuni and Pat

Translations From The Oriental Classics

PREFACE

Deliverance is not for me in renunciation.
I feel the embrace of freedom in a
thousand bonds of delight.

Rabindranath Tagore
Gitanjali 73

Jayadeva's dramatic lyrical poem *Gītagovinda* is a unique work in Indian literature and a source of religious inspiration in both medieval and contemporary Vaishnavism. The poem is dedicated in devotion to the god Krishna. It concentrates on Krishna's love with the cowherdess Rādhā in a rite of spring. Intense earthly passion is the example Jayadeva uses to express the complexities of divine and human love.

Although the poem originated in eastern India in the twelfth century and remains most popular there, it spread throughout the subcontinent in the centuries following its composition. As early as the thirteenth century it was quoted in a temple inscription in Gujarat, in western India. Established traditions of commentary and manuscripts exist in every part of India. Its songs are an important part of the devotional music and literature of Orissa, Bengal, and South India. The songs were introduced into Kerala in the sixteenth century and are still sung in temples there. Portions of the poem represent one of the major subjects in medieval Rājput painting.

Critical acclaim of the poem has been high, but its frank eroticism has led many Indian commentators to interpret the love between Rādhā and Krishna as an allegory of the human soul's love for God. The condemnation of Jayadeva's eroticism made by the seventeenth-century esthetician Jagannātha in his *Rasagaṅgādhara* (Kāvyamālā 12, Bombay, 1888, p. 52) is exceptional. Learned and popular audiences in India and elsewhere have continued to appreciate the emotional lyricism the poem expresses in its variations on the theme of separated lovers' passion.

Commenting on F. H. van Dalberg's German rendering of the *Gīta-govinda*, Goethe wrote, "What struck me as remarkable are the extremely varied motives by which an extremely simple subject is made endless" (note to Schiller dated Jan. 22, 1802, quoted from *Correspondence between Goethe and Schiller*, translated by L. D. Schmitz, London, 1909, vol. 2, p. 395). Dalberg's version was based on the first English translation of the *Gītagovinda* by William Jones, published in the *Transactions of the Asiatic Society, Calcutta*, in 1792 and reprinted in London in *Asiatik Researches*, 3 (1799), 185–207. A verse translation by the German poet Friedrich Rückert, begun in 1829 and revised according to the edited Sanskrit text and Latin translation of C. Lassen (Bonn, 1836), appeared in *Zeitschrift für die Kunde des Morgenlandes*, 1 (Gottingen, 1837), 128 ff.

The poem has also been translated into most modern Indian languages and many other modern European languages. Notable English versions include Edwin Arnold's *The Indian Song of Songs* (London, 1875); George Keyt's *Sri Jayadeva's Gita Govinda: The Loves of Kṛṣṇa and Rādhā* (Bombay, 1940); S. Lakshminarasimha Sastri's *The Gīta Govinda of Jayadeva* (Madras, 1956); Duncan Greenlees' Theosophical rendering, *The Song of Divine Love* (Madras, 1962), and Monica Varma's "trans-creation," *The Gita Govinda of Jayadeva*, published by Writers Workshop (Calcutta, 1968).

My own interest in the *Gītagovinda* began when I heard it sung in Orissi style in the home of Sulakshana and Debi Prasanna Pattanayak in Poona in 1966 and attempted to translate some of the songs. None of the available translations seemed to convey the literary richness or the religious significance of the original. My early work toward a verse translation of the poem convinced me that my English version should be based on a critical edition of the text and an extensive study of the traditions associated with the poem at various levels of Indian culture.

While I have concentrated my effort on textual aspects of the *Gīta-govinda*, I have also gathered and studied substantial material relevant to its cultural contexts. I have heard and recorded the songs of the poem in different musical versions in Orissa, Bengal, Bihar, Madras, Mysore, and Kerala, as well as Nepal. Because of the role of the songs in the nightly worship of the deity in Jagannātha Temple at Puri, they are venerated and sung throughout Orissa. Their performance is an essential aspect of Orissi dance, which has developed through the religious art of temple dancers called Maharis who still dance *Gītagovinda* songs before Jagannātha. The significance of the legendary life of Jayadeva that identifies the poet's muse as a temple dancer of Puri is discussed in the first section of my introduction. I have learned much about the emotional content of the poem from watching Sanjukta Panigrahi and Ritha Devi perform *Gītagovinda* songs in Orissi style. I spent many pleasant hours in Cuttack in consultation with Kalicharan Patnaik and Akshaya Mohanty discussing and listening to the music of *Gītagovinda*. A seventeenth-century palm-leaf manuscript of the text, with the commentary *Sarvāṅga-sundarī* and superb illustrations, was examined in the collection of Kalicharan.

In Bengal, the singing of *Gītagovinda* is especially prominent at an annual spring fair in the village of Kenduli in Birbhum district, which is identified as the birthplace of Jayadeva in Bengali tradition. The influence of the poem on the devotional music of Bengal is analyzed in an article by Swami Prajnananada entitled "The *Gītagovinda-padagāna* in the Background of the *Padāvalī-kīrtan* of Bengal," published in the *Journal of the Music Academy, Madras*, 36 (1965), 176–82.

In Nepal, the *Gītagovinda* is sung during the spring celebration in honor of the goddess Sarasvatī, in which worship is offered to the god of love, Kāmadeva, and his consort. I did not hear an actual performance, but learned about it in a talk with the father of my friend Dr. Prasanna Chandra Gautam, who read the description and chanted a portion of the poem from his brahman family's old manual of annual ceremonies, entitled *Vārṣikavratapaddhati*. In the Bir Library collection in the National Archives in Kathmandu, I found the earliest known manuscripts of the *Gītagovinda*, dated 567 and 616 in the Nepali era (ca. A.D. 1447 and 1496). Norvin Hein discusses the theatrical rendering of the *Gītagovinda* in regions where Śākta influence prevails, with special reference to its performance in Nepal and Bihar (*The Miracle Plays of Mathurā*, New Haven, 1972, pp. 267–71). He quotes the account of Sylvain Lévi of an evening performance by popular players in Kathmandu on March 7, 1898, in which the plot and songs were based on the *Gītagovinda*.

In much of South India the poem is sung according to the classical Karnatic system of music. An edition of the text with musical notation according to this system by Semmangudi R. Sreenivasa Iyer was published by the Sanskrit College Committee, Tripunithura, Kerala, in 1963. The text is prefaced by this note: "*Ashtapadi*, as the poem is popularly known, is sung daily in many of the temples of Kerala, as the pious Hindus consider it a devotional song of the highest order. It is also sung invariably during Kathakali performances, but the way of singing in

Kerala is different from that of Bhajanapaddhati which has been adopted by Mr. Sreenivasa Iyer." With the help of the music scholar K. P. S. Menon of Calicut, I was able to hear *Gītagovinda* songs as they are sung by members of a drummer caste in the courtyard of Guruvayur and other temples of Kerala while certain rituals are being performed by brahman priests within the sanctuary. Mr. Menon also provided me with an English text of Rama Varma's nineteenth-century version of the *Gītagovinda*, based on Kathakali technique. The Malayalam text, entitled *Ashtapadi Attaprakaram*, was edited by K. Raghavan Pillai and published in the Kerala University Malayalam Series (Trivandrum, 1964). The text came to my attention through a review of it by L. S. Rajagopalan in the *Journal of the Music Academy, Madras*, 37 (1966), 221–22. Mr. Rajagopalan's correspondence with me on the performance of the *Gītagovinda* in Kerala temples has provided many suggestions for further work on this subject.

In order to better understand the lyrical structure of the *Gītagovinda*, I have studied the theory and practice of both classical Hindusthani and classical Karnatic music. I studied the North Indian flute with Vasant Rai, a disciple of Allaudin Khan and the director of Alam School of North Indian Music in New York, and I took lessons on South Indian flute with V. Deshikachar at the Mysore College of Fine Arts. I have consulted a text of the *Gītagovinda* with annotations of the gestures (*abhinaya*) for every word in the first seventeen songs of the poem; this was edited by K. Vasudeva Sastri and published in the Tanjore Sarawati Mahal Series (Tanjore, 1950). Certain songs belong to the current repertoire of Bharata Natyam, and I relished the opportunity to watch and analyze some of these in the classes of Veṅkaṭalakshmyammā, also at the Mysore College of Fine Arts. These studies have informed my translation and analysis of the poem, but I have not attempted a technical discussion of its music and dance performances in deference to the excellent work by scholars in this area. In March 1967 Sangeet Natak Akademi and Lalit Kala Akademi sponsored a conference in New Delhi entitled "Geet Govind Celebrations." Published conference papers by C. S. Pant, Premlata Sharma, N. S. Ramachandran, Dilip Kumar Mukherjee, Rukmini Devi, and E. Nilakanta Singh analyze aspects of music and dance associated with the poem. Kapila Vatsyayan, author of the excellent book *Classical Indian Dance in Literature and the Arts* (New Delhi, 1968), is currently preparing an extensive study of the poem's expression in Indian music, dance, and the plastic arts. She presented a general paper on the subject at the International Sanskrit Conference in Delhi in 1972 that is scheduled for publication in the proceedings of that conference. Her analysis of the *Gītagovinda* in Manipuri dance, presented at the Manipur Sahitya Sangeet Natak Akademi in 1973, is being prepared for publication. My appreciation for the visual imagery of the *Gītagovinda* has been enhanced by published volumes of paintings from various schools. These include R. P. N. Sinha's *Geeta Govind in Basholi School of Indian Painting* (New Delhi, 1958); M.S. Randhawa's *Kangra Paintings of the Gītagovinda* (New Delhi, 1963); and Moti Chandra's two portfolios in the Lalit Kalā Series, both entitled *Gītagovinda* (New Delhi, 1965).

In my introduction, I have tried to analyze and trace the sources of formal and thematic elements that have been relevant to my understanding of Jayadeva's poetic creation. I have not tried to survey the wide influence of the poem on later Indian religious literature, poetry, and the arts. This material belongs to the study of Dr. Vatsyayan, whose published work promises to complement the present volume. The importance of the *Gītagovinda* in later Bengali Vaishnavism is well documented in the studies of Dasgupta, De, Dimock, and Harekrishna Mukhopādhyāya cited in the notes to sections two and three of the introduction. Its place in the broader development of Indian religious eroticism is central to a recent Oxford University doctoral thesis by Lee Siegel, entitled "Sacred and Profane Dimensions of Love in Indian Traditions as Exemplified in the *Gītagovinda* of Jayadeva" (Oxford, 1975). Several scholars have compiled descriptive lists of the literary imitations of the *Gītagovinda:* V. W. Karambelkar, "Three More Imitations of the *Gītagovinda,*" *Indian Historical Quarterly,* 25, no. 2 (1949), 95–101; K. N. Mahapatra, "Some Imitations of the Gītagovindam," *The Orissa Historical Research Journal,* 15, nos. 3 and 4 (1971), 95–130; V. Raghavan, "In the Footsteps of Jayadeva: Nanjaraja's *Saṅgīta Gaṅgādhara,*" unpublished typescript of 1972, revised from an article published in *The Hindu,* Madras, in 1936.

Documentation of my critical study of the *Gītagovinda* is presented, with the edited Sanskrit text, only in the hardcover edition of this book. It seemed unreasonable to increase the size of the paperback edition with material that would be of interest only to scholars. The hardcover edition also includes a glossary of Sanskrit words: this too is intended mainly for scholarly readers. Because the vocabulary of the poem is highly concentrated, the glossary serves as an alternative to repetitive textual notes. The translation is not directly annotated. I hope that the detailed discussions of the poem in various sections of the introduction will provide all that necessary for the general reader to enjoy and understand my

English version of Jayadeva's poetry. The discussions are supplemented by extensive bibliographic and textual notes. Because the bibliography differs so much from section to section, no general list of references is given. In preparing both the glossary and the introduction, as well as the translation itself, I have depended heavily on the interpretations and analyses of various commentators. The contents of selected commentaries are described as part of the evidence for the critical edition. References to variant interpretations of ambiguous phrases and technical terms are found in the glossary and the notes to the introduction.

The research for this book has taken me to India three times. My search for manuscripts in the summer of 1971 was supported by grants from the National Endowment for the Humanities and the American Philosophical Society. A grant from the American Council of Learned Societies enabled me to spend time in Madras and Orissa in January 1973 to consult manuscripts in the Adyar Library, the Orissa State Museum, and the Raghunandan Library, and to experience performances of the *Gītagovinda*. My residence at Mysore University during the winter of 1974–75 was supported by the American Institute of Indian Studies. A Guggenheim Fellowship for "A Textual and Contextual Study of Medieval Sanskrit Poetry and its Modern Interpretations" gave me time to consider the *Gītagovinda* in the broader context of medieval literature and to explore theories of the relationship between religion and art in Indian civilization. It also enabled me to work in Nepal in the autumn of 1974.

In the five years I have spent gathering and preparing the *Gītagovinda* material for publication, many people have given me invaluable help. My special thanks are to the Pattanayaks, who have often shared with me and my family the warmth and cultural life of their home. My formal affiliation at Mysore University was with the Central Institute of Indian Languages, of which Dr. Pattanayak is the director; the resources of the institute greatly facilitated my work. In Mysore, I was also helped by research scholars at the Oriental Institute and the Office of the Chief Epigraphist. I enjoyed many hours at the Oriental Institute discussing Sanskrit *kāvya* and analyzing aspects of the *Gītagovinda* with H. V. Nagaraja Rao. It was under his supervision that the Devanagari text of my critical edition was typeset at Sree Kantha Power Press, publishers of the Sanskrit newspaper *Sudharmā*. Without his gracious help, this book would not be in its present form. Thanks are due to Theodore Riccardi, Lynn Bennett, and Gabriel Campbell for their help in locating and identifying the Nepali materials that have been so central to my critical text;

and also to Neil Gross, who patiently collated the references for the glossary.

I am indebted to Daniel H. H. Ingalls for the example of his own work and for his encouragement of this translation through the endless revisions I submitted to his attention. For their generous and detailed criticism at various stages of the translation, I thank Susan Bergholz, Edwin Gerow, Jeffrey Masson, Agueda Pizarro, David Rubin, Burton Watson, and my husband James. William Bernhardt, Karen Mitchell, and Andrée Mounier of Columbia University Press have all contributed to the conception and form of the book; I appreciate their skills and standards.

James and Gwenn have shared my travels in the Indian subcontinent and much of my adventure in studying the *Gitagovinda*. Their appreciation for the music of Jayadeva's poem and for my involvement with it have made this work pleasurable.

Barbara Stoler Miller

NEW YORK, 1976

CONTENTS

A NOTE ON SANSKRIT PRONUNCIATION

In reading Sanskrit words, the accent is usually placed on the penultimate syllable when this is long; otherwise it is placed on the antepenultimate. A syllable is long if it contains a long vowel (*ā, ī, ū*), a diphthong (*e, o, ai, au*), or a vowel followed by more than one consonant. It should be noted that the aspirated consonants *ḳh, gh, ch, jh, th, dh, ph, bh,* and so on are considered single consonants in the Sanskrit alphabet.

Vowels are given their full value, as in Italian or German:

a   as *u* in c*u*t
ā   as *a* in f*a*ther
i   as *i* in p*i*t
ī   as *i* in mach*i*ne
u   as *u* in p*u*t
ū   as *u* in r*u*le
ṛ   a short vowel; as *ri* in *ri*ver
e   as *ay* in s*ay*
ai as *ai* in *ai*sle
o   as *o* in g*o*
au as *ow* in c*ow*
ṁ   nasalizes and lengthens the preceding vowel
ḥ   a rough breathing, replacing an original *s* or *r;* lengthens the preceding vowel and occurs only at the end of a syllable or word

Most consonants are analogous to the English, if the distinction between aspirated and nonaspirated consonants is observed; for example, the aspirated consonants *th* and *ph* must never be pronounced as in English *th*in and *ph*ial, but as in ho*th*ouse and she*ph*erd. (Similarly, *ḳh, gh, ch, jh, dh, bh.*) The differences between the Sanskrit "cerebral" *ṭ, ṭh, ḍ, ḍh, ṇ,* and "dental" *t, th, d, dh, n* are another distinctive feature of the language. The dentals are formed with the tongue against the teeth, the cerebrals with the tongue turned back along the palate. Note also:

g   as *g* in *g*oat
ṅ   as *n* in i*n*k, or si*ng*
c   as *ch* in *ch*urch

ñ   as *ñ* in se*ñ*or (Spanish)

ś, ṣ   as *sh* in *sh*ape or *s* in *s*ugar.

Kṛṣṇa and Viṣṇu are spelled Krishna and Vishnu for the convenience of the reader.

Introduction

1 Jayadeva: The Wandering Poet

> Jayadeva, wandering king of bards
> Who sing at Padmāvatī's lotus feet,
> Was obsessed in his heart
> By rhythms of the goddess of speech,
> And he made this lyrical poem
> From tales of the passionate play
> When Krishna loved Śrī.

———◆·◆———

Jayadeva, the poet's signature in the *Gītagovinda,* is the name by which he is known as a poet-saint in Indian tradition.[1] It is a name he shares with Krishna, the divine hero of his poem; he invokes Krishna in the second song with the refrain *jaya jayadeva hare,* "Triumph, God of Triumph, Hari!" In the context where the poet's name becomes an epithet of Krishna, the name in turn gains a dimension of sacred meaning. The listener is reminded of Jayadeva's special relation to Krishna as his name is repeated in the signature verse that ends each song.

The lyrical, religious eroticism of the *Gītagovinda* earned sainthood for Jayadeva and a wide audience for his poem. All versions of the legend that sanctifies Jayadeva's life say that he was born in a brahman family and that he became an accomplished student of Sanskrit and a skilled poet.[2] However, he abandoned scholarship at a young age and adopted an ascetic life, devoting himself to God. As a wandering mendicant, he would not rest under one tree for more than a night for fear that attachment to the place would violate his vow. His ascetic life ended when a brahman of Puri insisted that Jagannātha, "Lord of the World," himself had ordained the marriage of Jayadeva with the brahman's daughter Padmāvatī, who was dedicated as a dancing girl in the temple. Padmāvatī served her husband and he shared her devotion to Jagannātha. As Jayadeva composed, she danced—thus the *Gītagovinda.* In the process of writing the poem, Jayadeva conceived the climax of Krishna's supplication to Rādhā as a command for Rādhā to place her foot on Krishna's head in a symbolic gesture of victory (X.8). But the poet hesitated to complete the couplet, in deference to Krishna. He went to bathe and in his absence

———◆·◆———

Krishna appeared in his guise to write the couplet; then Krishna ate the food Padmāvatī had prepared for Jayadeva and left. When Jayadeva returned, he realized that he had received divine grace in exalting Krishna's loving relation to Rādhā.

Various local versions of this legend have grown into conflicting traditions about Jayadeva's place of birth and region of poetic activity. Modern scholars of Bengal, Orissa, and Mithila have put forth claims locating the village of his birth in their respective regions. Two strong traditions say that the "Kindubilva" cited in the Gītagovinda (III.10) is either a village near Puri in Orissa or a village in the modern Birbhum district of Bengal. A third tradition identifies the village of Kenduli near Jenjharpur in Mithila as Jayadeva's birthplace. The argument is well known and has been summarized in favor of Jayadeva's Bengali origins in a recent monograph by Suniti Kumar Chatterji.[3] Although the Bengali position remains tenuous, both legends and historical documents suggest that Jayadeva lived and composed in eastern India during the latter half of the twelfth century.

The dating of Jayadeva's literary activity is established by the composite evidence of various literary and historical documents. Most prominent is the presence of verses attributed to Jayadeva in Śrīdharadāsa's Saduktikarṇāmṛta, an anthology compiled in Bengal in A.D. 1205 (Śāka era 1127), at the end of the reign of Lakṣmaṇasena, who ruled about A.D. 1179–1205.[4] Among the thirty verses attributed to Jayadeva in S. C. Banerji's edition of the anthology, two are in the critical text of the Gītagovinda.[5] In the Gītagovinda (I.3), Jayadeva compares himself with poets named Umāpatidhara, Śaraṇa, Govardhana, and Dhoyī,[6] all of whom are quoted in the Saduktikarṇāmṛta. Dhoyī composed a court epic entitled Pavanadūta, "Wind-messenger," to glorify a campaign by Lakṣmaṇasena into the south.[7] The other poets are less directly associated with Lakṣmaṇasena, but their works relate them to the period and region of his reign.[8]

It seems clear from the contents of the Saduktikarṇāmṛta and from the inscriptions of Lakṣmaṇasena that the king was a patron of Sanskrit learning and of Vaishnavism. The Senas were Karnatic kings who employed Sanskrit for their official documents, the standard practice in North India at this time.[9] The inscriptions of Lakṣmaṇasena open with an invocation to Vishnu (auṁ auṁ namo nārāyaṇāya) instead of to Śiva, as had been the practice of his predecessors. The king is described by the epithet "Highest Vaishnava" (paramavaiṣṇava).[10] A court that promoted Sanskrit learning and the highly syncretic Vaishnava worship of this time would have provided an appreciative audience for the *Gītagovinda*. It is impossible to know whether Jayadeva composed the work at Lakṣmaṇasena's court; perhaps he composed it elsewhere and performed it there. The South Indian Vaishnava devotional cults that were influential in Bengal in the twelfth century were equally active in Orissa. Traditional accounts record that Rāmānuja, the great Vedānta philosopher and apostle of the Śrīvaishnava cult, visited Puri in the early part of the twelfth century and established a school there. It is claimed that he met and influenced the King of Puri and worked to introduce the ritual of Śrīvaishnavism into the Jagannātha temple, against the strong opposition of resident Śaiva priests.[11] The king whom he met was probably Anantavarman Choḍagaṅgadeva, the Gaṅga king who ruled in Orissa about A.D. 1078–1147. Later Gaṅga records suggest that Choḍagaṅgadeva initiated major construction of the Jagannātha temple, which was completed during the reign of his grandson Anaṅgabhīmadeva in the late twelfth century. From the evidence of his inscriptions, Choḍagaṅgadeva, like Lakṣmaṇasena of Bengal, came under Vaishnava influence. Two sets of copperplate inscriptions illustrate the shift in his sectarian allegiance. In A.D. 1081 (Śāka era 1003), Choḍagaṅgadeva expressed traditional Gaṅga devotion to Śiva by granting land to support worship of *Rājarājeśvara,* a name of Śiva. In A.D. 1118 (Śāka era 1040), in a grant of land to a brahman named Mādhava, his inscription begins with an invocation to Lakṣmī, and the king is described as "Highest Vaishnava" (*paramavaiṣṇava*). Temple records show that since the time of Choḍagaṅgadeva, Jagannātha has been continuously worshipped as the supreme form of Vishnu, whose power is expressed through the energy of his consort, Lakṣmī or Śrī.[12]

Although the legend of Jayadeva's life has no historical value, it does tell us that in the course of his wanderings Jayadeva visited Puri, where he came under the influence of the Jagannātha cult and formed a special relationship with Padmāvatī. The identification of Padmāvatī as Jayadeva's wife is not supported by either of the early commentators on the *Gītagovinda.* Both Mānāṅka and Kumbhakarṇa identify *Padmāvatī* (I.2; X.9; XI.21), or *Padmā* (I.25), as names of Krishna's divine consort *Śrī* (I.2; I.23), or *Lakṣmī* (XI.22), who is also called *Kamalā* (I.17) in the poem. The "marriage" of Jayadeva and Padmāvatī in the legend may be a veiled allusion to his initiation in the Śrīvaishnava cult that was established in Puri under Rāmānuja's influence. The role of Krishna's cowherdess consort Rādhā in the *Gītagovinda* takes its cosmic significance from the context of recurrent references to Śrī. Jayadeva's use of the epithet *Jagadīśa,* "Lord of the World," for Krishna in the first song is too similar to *Jagannātha* to be accidental—the *Gītagovinda* may well have taken shape in the richly syncretic environment in Puri in the twelfth century.[13]

By the fifteenth century, the *Gītagovinda* was sufficiently popular in Puri to be incorporated into the ritual of the Jagannātha temple. An inscription located on the left side of the Jayavijaya doorway, written in Oriya language and script and dated A.D. 1499, prescribes the performance of the *Gītagovinda* in the temple.[14] An English translation of the inscription reads:

> On Wednesday the tenth lunar year of Kakaḍā, bright half in the ninth mark of the warrior, the elephant-lord, the mighty Pratāparudradeva Mahārāja, king over Gauḍa and the ninety millions of Karṇāta and Kalabaraga, orders as follows: "Dancing will be performed thus at the time of food-offerings (*bhoga*) to the Elder Lord (Balarāma) and the Lord of the *Gītagovinda* (Jagannātha). This dancing will continue from the end of the deities' evening meal to their bedtime meal. The dancing group of the Elder Lord, the female dancers of Lord Kapileśvara, and the ancient dancing group of Telangana will all learn no song other than the *Gītagovinda* from the Elder Lord. *Aum.* They will sing no other song. No other dance should be performed before the great God. In addition to the dancing, there will be four singers who will sing only the *Gītagovinda.* Those who are not versed in singing the *Gītagovinda* will follow in chorus—they should learn no other song. Any temple official who knowingly allows any other song or dance to be performed is hostile to Jagannātha."

In the early sixteenth century, the great Vaishnava mystic Caitanya made a pilgrimage to Puri and settled there. It is recorded in the spiritual biography of Caitanya by Kṛṣṇadāsa Kavirāja, entitled *Caitanyacaritāmṛta,* that Caitanya derived great joy from hearing the *Gītagovinda,* as well as the songs of the Bengali poet Caṇḍīdāsa and the Maithili poet Vidyāpati.[15] There is no reference to the origin of Caitanya's devotion to the songs of the *Gītagovinda,* but it is likely that he heard them in the temple of Jagannātha. His love for Jayadeva's songs led to the canonization of the *Gītagovinda* within the Vaishnava Sahajiyā cult and its interpretation according to the doctrines of Bengali Vaishnavism.[16] Sahajiyā tradition claims Jayadeva as a practicer of its unorthodox ritual and the "original preceptor" (*ādiguru*) of the cult.[17] Jayadeva's ritual practice is not revealed by his poem, but the place of his songs in the Caitanya cult complements the Oriya tradition that nightly performance of the songs in worship of Jagannātha at Puri has been continuous for more than seven hundred years.[18]

By the end of the thirteenth century, the *Gītagovinda* was known in western India. A stone inscription of Mahārāja Sāraṅgadeva Vāghelā of Aṇahillapattan, dated A.D. 1291 (Vikrama era 1348), opens with Jayadeva's invocation to Krishna in his ten incarnate forms (I.16).[19] The inscription records the levying of a revised tax on the inhabitants of Pālhanapura (modern Palanpur) to defray the expenses of temple offerings to Krishna. The *Gītagovinda* was probably brought to Gujarat by Vaishnava pilgrims who heard it at Puri or some other eastern center of the Krishna cult.

Further evidence of the poem's wide dissemination in the centuries following its composition includes the existence of one palm-leaf manuscript in Newari hooked characters dated ca. A.D. 1447 (Nepali era 567) and another in Newari script dated ca. A.D. 1496 (Nepali era 616).[20] The text of this version accords well with the text on which Mānāṅka based his simple commentary. The fifteenth-century date given to an early paper manuscript of the *Gītagovinda*, accompanied by Mānāṅka's commentary and illustrated with paintings of the ten incarnations of Krishna in the Gujarati style of the mid-fifteenth century, is corroborated by the date, ca. A.D. 1512 (*saṁvat* 1569), on another manuscript of Mānāṅka's commentary.[21] The literary critical commentary of Kumbhakarṇa, called *Rasikapriyā*, is dated the mid-fifteenth century according to the dates of the ruler of Mewar named Kumbhakarṇa (A.D. 1433–68), with whom the commentator is identified.[22] By the sixteenth century Jayadeva's poem was recognized throughout northern India for the intensity of its poetic and its religious expression.

2 *The Lyrical Structure of Jayadeva's Poem*

The *Gītagovinda*, deceptively simple in its surface beauty, has a wealth of meaning embedded in structurally intricate forms and concepts drawn from various levels of Indian literary tradition. In the process of preparing this textual analysis and translation, I have come to appreciate how masterfully Jayadeva interwove formal and thematic elements to create a work of high art and religious intensity that remains appealing to popular audiences throughout the Indian subcontinent. In order to translate the lyric drama into an English form that conveys its sense and characteristic texture, I have found it essential to unravel these elements, trace their sources, and understand how Jayadeva used them in his own innovative ways.

I have tried to find a diction within current English that would be receptive to the letters, words, meanings, and textures of Jayadeva's Sanskrit—a medium in which the translation could become a representation of the original. The choice has not been between translation of words (*śabdānuvāda*) and translation of feeling (*bhāvānuvāda*). Words derive meaning from the contexts in which they occur. Words in their various levels of denotative, connotative, and suggested meanings, as well as in their grammatical forms and structural relations, are the stuff out of which feeling is made in poetry. To paraphrase I. A. Richards, word and feeling are interlinked so closely that to dissect one from the other is a perilous operation.[1] Word and feeling have functioned inseparably in the translation process. Critical analysis of Jayadeva's language, style, and concepts has helped to integrate these throughout.[2]

In Sanskrit literature creative expression was circumscribed by strict conventions, which served to expand the significance of words and images beyond their given meaning. Sanskrit poets sought to awaken response by manipulating complex language, figures of speech, and imagery in skillful improvisation. Classical poets like Kālidāsa and Bhartṛhari appealed exclusively to an educated audience of men who were familiar with poetic techniques and were capable of understanding the linguistic subtleties of Sanskrit grammar.[3] Jayadeva seems to have been consciously appealing to a more diverse audience, characterized by broader literary taste and religious devotion. Verses in the *Gītagovinda* (e.g., I.2, 4; XII.22) express the poet's intent to reach an audience sympathetic to the creative purpose of enjoying Krishna's divine love through esthetic experience.

Jayadeva seems to have searched the literary expressions of his poetic heritage and contemporary experience to distill a genre appropriate to his vision of Krishna's springtime rite of love. The form of the *Gītagovinda* defies categorization in any classical genre of Sanskrit literature. The lyricism and dramatic movement of the poem may be based on some non-classical form, but the complex structures Jayadeva uses to integrate religious, erotic, and esthetic meaning suggest that his inspiration for the *Gītagovinda* also came from works like Kālidāsa's classical epic, the *Kumārasambhava*, "The Birth of the Prince," and the same author's unique lyric poem, the *Meghadūta*, "The Cloud-messenger."[4] Jayadeva's application to Sanskrit of elaborate sound patterns of rhyme, alliteration, and measured rhythm offers concrete evidence of how he used techniques of "popular" songs to exploit the lyric potential of the classical language.[5]

The *Gītagovinda* is best characterized as a dramatic lyrical poem. It is expressed as a cycle of songs [6] interspersed with recitative portions in the metrical forms of classical *kāvya* verses. These *kāvya* verses function as independent grammatical and esthetic entities. Most of them are narrative verses identifying the singer of a song or elaborating its context. Others, like verse I.47, are relatively independent of the story and serve primarily to reinforce the esthetic atmosphere of the poem. Such verses may be recalled and enjoyed like miniature paintings from an album.

> Winds from sandalwood mountains
> Blow now toward Himalayan peaks,
> Longing to plunge in the snows
> After weeks of writhing
> In the hot bellies of ground snakes.
> Melodious voices of cuckoos
> Raise their joyful sound
> When they spy the buds
> On tips of smooth mango branches.

The brief *kāvya* verses in the *Gītagovinda* may contain dense descriptions and complex ideas. Classical ornamentation (*alaṁkāra*) is used to expand meaning. Alliterations and sensuous vocabulary, which are general characteristics of the songs, occur in some verses. Subtle forms of metaphor (*upamā*) employed in the verses are recognized by the commentators.[7]

Since contrasting metrical patterns are basic to the structure of the *Gītagovinda,* the distinction between syllabic meter (*akṣaravṛtta*) and two types of moric meter (*tālavṛtta*) must be recognized.[8] The basic patterns of both syllabic and moric meters depend on the quantity of individual syllables in a unit of verse. Syllabic meters are generally characterized by fixed sequences of short, or "light," and long, or "heavy," syllables repeated in each quarter of a verse. The musical moric meters are defined by the number of beats (*mātra*) in a line, with each light syllable counting as one beat and each heavy syllable as two beats. Most moric meters are further patterned into measures (*gaṇa*), the most common type being a measure of four beats (*caturgaṇa*).

Within the seventy-two *kāvya* verses included in the critical edition of the *Gītagovinda,* twelve different syllabic meters occur.[9] There are also three verses in the moric meter Āryā (VI.1; VII.2; IX.1). Āryā is the most extensively used moric meter in Sanskrit poetry. It is the characteristic meter of poetry in Prākrit dialects of the classical period, exemplified by the contents of Hāla's anthology, the *Sattasaī,*[10] and by Prākrit verses in Sanskrit dramas. Although the classical Āryā meter is organized in terms of beat and measure, like the songs of the *Gītagovinda,* its formal articulation makes it distinct from the types of measured meters that order the songs.[11]

In comparison with the compact form and contained grammar of the classical *kāvya* verses, the structure of the songs is broader and more complex. A composite pattern of three interdependent formal units is repeated in each of the twenty-four songs.[12] The fixed unit in each song is the *dhruvapada,* a "refrain" that is repeated after each couplet; it is the stable unit of sound and meaning in the song. Its content provides a context for the descriptive details of the couplets and intensifies their meaning. Where the *dhruvapada* contains the grammatical subject to which descriptive compounds and phrases refer, it resolves the "dangling" syntax of the couplets. The refrains are characterized by syntactic simplicity and a core vocabulary of recurring words that suggest correspondences between Rādhā and Krishna at different stages of their separation. Just as a refrain unifies a song, the network of refrains unifies the poem.

The varying unit in each song is the *pada,* a stanza that is one of a series of rhymed couplets occuring in a particular moric metrical pattern. From this comes the designation of the songs as *padāvalī,* "stanza-series," a term that Jayadeva introduces in the *Gītagovinda* (I.4). Since the stanzas usually number eight, the songs are also referred to as *aṣṭapadī,* "eight-stanza song."

The final formal unit is the *bhaṇita,* the last *pada* in each song. Each *bhaṇita* repeats the poet's signature, Jayadeva, and usually some form of the root √*bhaṇ,* which means "saying" or "singing." This stanza reaffirms the affinities of the poet's creative activity and the audience's esthetic experience to the developing erotic relationship between Rādhā and Krishna. It functions in each song to give the perspective of esthetic and religious perception to the emotional intensity of the preceding stanzas and the refrain.

The system of moric meters in the *Gītagovinda* songs gives the poem its rhythmical structure. A particular meter relates couplets within a song, and the metrical system relates the songs to one another. Jayadeva's skillful variation of a few selected metrical patterns sustains the aural appeal of his long poem.

As I have already suggested, the moric meters of the songs contrast with the traditional moric meters like Āryā in several ways. The severely restricted occurrence of heavy syllables is most striking. Heavy syllables are relatively rare in the songs; they are limited mainly to initial position within the *gaṇa* units and to the ends of lines. This gives the songs their lilting quality and definite rhythmical beat. The rhythmical element is further emphasized by repetitious sound patterns of alliteration, assonance, consonance, and end rhyme. These devices are all used in earlier Sanskrit literature, but nowhere else with the persistence that characterizes the *Gītagovinda*.

The meters of the songs and the mode of their articulation clearly resemble the meters of medieval poetry in the vernacular languages known as Apabhraṁśa. Although few of Jayadeva's meters are specifically identifiable with those known from either Jain Apabhraṁśa poetry of western India or Buddhist Caryāpada poetry of eastern India, the predominant metrical pattern of the songs corresponds with the basic rhythmic design of such non-Sanskrit medieval poetry. The correspondence had led scholars like Pischel, Renou, and Chatterji to suggest that the songs, or even the entire poem, were originally composed in Apabhraṁśa and then translated into Sanskrit.[13] A close reading of the songs and a comparison of the songs with the *kāvya* verses in the poem suggest instead that Jayadeva adapted the musical moric meters of vernacular poetry in order to create a medium of song within conventional poetic Sanskrit. If one analyzes Jayadeva's style in terms of meter, ornamentation, and structure, the classical elements drawn from Sanskrit and Prākrit sources are as significant to the songs as the Apabhraṁśa meters. Jayadeva's adaptation of Apabhraṁśa meters to Sanskrit is not an isolated phenomenon. It is the most sustained and successful of several such experiments that are known from the tenth century and after, when the bonds of classical Sanskrit literature were loosened by attempts to broaden its appeal.[14]

The most prominent meter in the *Gītagovinda* songs repeats a pattern of couplets structured into lines of seven four-beat measures, exemplified by the opening couplet of the third song (I.27):[15]

lalitala|vaṅgala|tāpari|śīlana|komala|malayasa|mīre|
madhukara|nikaraka|rambita|kokila|kūjita|kuñjaku|ṭire ||

This meter and its variants, which maintain the four-beat measure, govern nineteen of the twenty-four songs in the *Gītagovinda*.[16] The dominant metrical unit of the songs reflects the four-beat subdivision of the most common rhythmical pattern (*tāla*) of both Hindusthani and Karnatic classical music. The meter of a song can provide the rhythmical component of the song's music. It seems significant that no *tāla* designations are given in two of the oldest manuscripts of the *Gītagovinda*, though each song in these manuscripts is defined by the name of a melodic pattern (*rāga*). Where *tāla* names do accompany *rāga* names in other manuscripts, there is enormous variability with regard to the *tāla* names.[17]

Most of the refrains are in moric metrical patterns that maintain the same measured beat as that of the associated couplets.[18] They generally contrast with the couplets in length only. Refrains usually consist of one line or two rhyming lines of unequal length. The rhythmic cadences of the refrains tend to be heavier than those of the couplets, thus giving their words greater emphasis.[19]

Rhyme, in its several varieties, highlights the rhythmic patterns of the songs. Alliteration (*anuprāsa*) in Sanskrit poetry involves the echo of repeated sounds in a line; it is not limited to the initial sounds of words. Alliteration is the rhyming device most commonly used to produce emphasis and euphony in classical *kāvya*.[20] In the *Gītagovinda* alliterative combinations of consonants and vowels reinforce the meters and the sensuous imagery of the songs. They often contribute to the rhythmical complexity of a line by forcing syllables into a syncopation of the metrical accent.[21]

End-rhyme (*antānuprāsa*) is a universal feature of the couplets. It serves to mark the close of each metrical cycle. This consistent use of end-rhyme is rare in classical Sanskrit poetry, though internal rhyme is common, as it is in the *kāvya* verses of the *Gītagovinda*.[22]

The eminent critic Ānandavardhana warns that a poet's preoccupation with repetitions of sound, like word-play, alliteration, and assonance, is an obstacle to the production of erotic mood.[23] But most Sanskrit critics consider these devices essential to the sweetness of poetry (*madhura, mādhurya*).[24] These critics seem to agree with the practicing poets that sense and sound must complement each other to create intensity in the expression of erotic mood.

The entire *Gītagovinda* abounds in various forms of word-play as well as rhyme. The repetition and shifting meaning of key words like *rasa* (taste), *madhu* (honey), and *vilāsa* (seduction), relate levels of content within the poem and often expand the context of a verse or song. Jayadeva puns on the names of certain meters he uses in the *kāvya* verses.[25] He plays on the names of heavenly nymphs to describe Rādhā (X.14). He plays on the epithets of Krishna, especially *Mādhava, Madhusūdana,* and *Hari.* The poet's own name, Jayadeva, which is also used as an epithet of Krishna, is repeated as the poet's signature at the end of each song.[26]

The grammar of the songs is simplified. Certain forms are repeated frequently. Prominent are the locative, which is often used in its absolute function, the instrumental, and various participles. In the tenth song, unvarying grammatical parallelism governs each of the couplets.

In the *Gītagovinda* repetitive patterns of sounds, syllables, words, and phrases serve to reinforce and supplement the metrical structures of the songs. All Sanskrit poetry contains generous amounts of sound elaboration (*śabdālaṁkāra*); [27] in the songs of the *Gītagovinda* the redundancies are incessant, complex, and multileveled. They create a sensuous surface of verbal ornamentation that suggests comparison with the sculptured surfaces of the medieval Hindu temples of Bhubaneswar and Khajuraho. In the rhythmic disposition of a basic ground plan and the superimposition of repetitive shapes along a vertical axis, each temple moves to a point of intense concentration, where it simultaneously plunges into the womb-house of the deity and transcends itself.[28] The intricate vertical and horizontal design that emerges in the *Gītagovinda* from the repetitions of metrical units, refrains, rhymes, alliterations, technical words, puns, and syntactic devices unifies the entire poem and concentrates its movement.

All known manuscripts of the *Gītagovinda* indicate the names of various *rāgas,* or melodic patterns, for individual songs. The Indian *rāga* is a melodic formula that includes particular embellishments and tone colors. The technique of improvisation, which is essential to the formal presentation of a *rāga,* uses dense combinations of grace notes and microtonal ornaments. The *rāga,* in the form of either a song or an instrumental piece, is identifiable in performance by its characteristic turns of phrase and dominant tones. In theory, every *rāga* is associated with a particular mood, time, and seasonal setting.[29]

The songs of the *Gītagovinda* are sung in regions of eastern and southern India in a variety of different *rāgas.*[30] Although the oldest manuscripts show striking agreement in designating a group of eleven different *rāgas* for the twenty-four songs, there has been no traditional transmission or notation to assure that these names designate the same melodic patterns they do in later times. The fact that many commentators are preoccupied with defining the *rāgas* in terms of Indian music theory suggests that the songs were variously interpreted throughout their history.

3 Jayadeva's Language for Love

Poetry is distinguished from ordinary modes of speech by the controlled and stylized ways it strives to transcend the limits of ordinary language. The lyrical techniques of Jayadeva's songs combine with the conventional language of Sanskrit erotic poetry to express the intimate power of divine love.[1] As Jayadeva's elaborates the passion of Rādhā and Krishna, he creates an esthetic atmosphere of erotic mood (*śṛṅgārarasa*) that is bliss for devotees of Krishna. The poet's aim is implied in an opening verse of the *Gītagovinda* (I.4):

> If remembering Hari enriches your heart,
> If his arts of seduction arouse you,
> Listen to Jayadeva's speech
> In these sweet soft lyrical songs.

The relation between esthetic and spiritual experience is made explicit in the signature verse of the final song of the poem (XII.19):

> Make your heart sympathetic to Jayadeva's splendid speech!
> Recalling Hari's feet is elixir against fevers of this dark time.
> She told the joyful Yadu hero, playing to delight her heart.

The concept of mood, *rasa*, is at the heart of all Indian artistic expression. *Rasa* is literally the taste or flavor of something. The *rasa* of a verse, song, dramatic scene, or musical performance is the flavor of a pervading emotion (*sthāyibhāva*). Sanskrit poets and critics came to realize the unique power and the esthetic potential of sexual passion (*ratibhāva*) in its aspects of pain and pleasure.[2] The erotic mood that emerges from passion was expressed in the antithetical modes of "separation" (*vipralambhaśṛṅgāra*) and "consummation" (*saṁbhogaśṛṅgāra*). To experience this mood in the interplay of its two modes was considered the height of esthetic joy.[3] Jayadeva created the religiously potent atmosphere of the *Gītagovinda* by exploring the poignant mood of separation within the broader play of divine passion in consummation.

Passion is transformed into erotic mood when a poet distills essential qualities from the confusion of spontaneous emotion and then patterns them according to universalizing rules of composition. Passion is made palpable through sensuous descriptions of movements and physical forms. Seasonal changes in nature and bodily signs of inner feeling are colored richly to create a dense atmosphere of passion.[4] The theorists dictated that the gestures exposing a character's mental states must be subtle, expressive enough to arouse a sensitive audience but never so crudely detailed that they stimulate wanton desire.[5] In the *Gītagovinda*, this restraint functions to make potentially pornographic subject matter the material of esthetic and religious experience.

In Jayadeva's environment of springtime (*sarasavasanta*, I.27 *), Rādhā and Krishna are vehicles (*vibhāva*) for the universalization of erotic emotion. These youthful figures with gleaming flesh and lotus-petal eyes manifest signs of emotion (*vyabhicāribhāva, sāttvikabhāva*) to communicate the passion of their separation. For Jayadeva, their longing and reunion is the concrete example of religious experience in which the disquieting distinction between "I" and "mine" verses "you" and "yours" is calmed.[6] The esthetic experience of their love is the means for breaking the imaginary barrier dividing human from divine.

The poet's direct presence throughout the poem dramatizes his view that the discipline of esthetic perception is a way to enjoy Krishna's graceful love. Each signature verse is a variation on the idea that the emotional states of Rādhā and Krishna have religious power through the medium of the poet's lyric presentation.

Insight into Jayadeva's conception is found by following the way he presents his characters through the movement of the poem's twelve parts. After evoking Rādhā and Krishna in their secret erotic relationship and stating his own aim, Jayadeva invokes the ten cosmic incarnations of Krishna. He proceeds to present increasingly intimate aspects of Krishna's relation to existence, focusing on the suffering he shares with Rādhā in the frustration of their love. Krishna's ecstatic reunion with Rādhā within the forest thicket in springtime allows the poet's audience to witness the center of existence. The vision (*darśana*) of Krishna revealed through Rādhā at the end of the poem is a vision of the soul of his erotic mood (*ekarasa*, XI.24–31, song 22). Its effect is comparable with Krishna's manifestation to Arjuna in the eleventh chapter of the *Bhagavadgītā*. Rādhā's heart, strengthened by the long trial of their separation and by the force of Krishna's suffering, is filled with erotic mood (*sarasamanas*, XII.1) that is the consummation (*saṁbhogaśṛṅgāra*) of the erotic, esthetic, religious experience Jayadeva creates for himself and his audience. This vision is contained within the structure of the poem, like the vision that climaxes a worshipper's controlled approach to the deity in the womb of a Hindu temple. On another level, the poetic perspective follows the movement of Rādhā's friend (*sakhī*), who goes between the parted lovers to describe the condition of each to the other. This perspective begins on Rādhā's side, but it subtly shifts to mediate between Rādhā and Krishna and bring them into union. The friend, the poet, and the audience share the experience of secretly participating in the play of divine love.[7]

The *Gītagovinda* begins with a classical verse indicating the subject of the poem.[8]

> "Clouds thicken the sky.
> Tamāla trees darken the forest.
> The night frightens him.
> Rādhā, you take him home!"
> They leave at Nanda's order,
> Passing trees in thickets on the way,
> Until secret passions of Rādhā and Mādhava
> Triumph on the Jumna riverbank.

The place, the time, the characters, and their relationship in the poem are superficially clear in this verse. But details of the episode are rich in symbolism and have encouraged complicated interpretations of Jayadeva's meaning.[9] Most interpretations turn on the identification of the speaker of the first half of the verse and on the reference to Krishna's "fear" and Rādhā's role as his guide through the dark forest. The opening speech is variously attributed to Krishna,[10] Rādhā,[11] Nanda,[12] or even the friend of Rādhā.[13] Jayadeva is characteristically ambiguous here—the many voices that are possible in the verse all direct the sexual energies of Krishna toward Rādhā, but each voice slightly shifts the quality of the darkness and of Krishna's fear. When we hear Krishna's foster-father, the cowherd-chief Nanda, address Rādhā, Krishna's youthful fear of the dark is suggested. When we hear Rādhā speaking to herself, the words suggest a woman sensing the sexual fear of her adolescent lover. When we hear Krishna himself speaking he is courting Rādhā in the veiled language of love, where feigned fear is a device of seduction. The composite voice further suggests that fear may relate to the cosmic age of darkness, the Kali Yuga, for which the union of Rādhā and Krishna is the cure.[14]

The darkness of the night in the forest is described in voluptuous sounds and imagery that echo through the entire poem.[15] It is in this secret, sexually stimulating environment that Krishna and Rādhā enact the initial triumph of their divine love and then suffer the long night of separation that ends in their reunion. They follow the path through the forest as a pair, which Jayadeva calls Rādhā-Mādhava.[16] The triumph of their passions occurs in this dual state, which is the defining structure of their relationship in the *Gītagovinda*. The "home" to which Rādhā brings Krishna is a forest thicket (*kuñja*), the secret place of their divine love, in which they meet again at the end of their journey.

The erotic mysticism of the *Gītagovinda*, which inspired the Vaishnava saint Caitanya, was interpreted allegorically by Caitanya's followers in terms of the Sahajiyā doctrine of devotional esthetics (*bhaktirasa*);[17] they used love as a metaphor whose primary reference was a metaphysical conception. Although many elements in the *Gītagovinda* are codified in the Sahajiyā doctrine of love, this reading seems artificial. Jayadeva's verses nowhere praise unbodied joy; they are explicitly sensual, and celebrate the sensual joy of divine love. Through imagery, tone color, and rhythm, Jayadeva interweaves levels of physical and metaphysical associations, and the cosmic energy of Krishna's love with Rādhā is condensed into a religious ecstasy.

4 Krishna: Cosmic Cowherd Lover

Krishna's mythology is ancient and complicated, emerging in the earliest levels of the epic *Mahābhārata* and developing through the various phases of Purānic literature. The history and significance of the Krishna legend has been analyzed in numerous scholarly studies; the summary that follows borrows freely from them.[1]

The process of Krishna's deification is discernible in epic literature. In the accounts of him in the *Mahābhārata* and the *Harivaṁśa*, his character is a transparent composite of a cowherd hero and a tribal chief who is also a form, or an incarnation (*avatāra*), of the god Vishnu. The mundane and cosmic levels of his activity are interwoven in the narratives to encompass elements from various sources in a complex mythic structure.[2] The basic account includes Krishna's miraculous birth, his concealment among cowherds to protect him from his demonic uncle Kaṁsa, his child-hood pranks and miraculous deeds in the cowherds' village, his youthful sexual play in the forest with the cowherdesses of Vraja, his destruction of demons, his defeat and killing of Kaṁsa, his role in the Bhārata war as the cunning and unscrupulous counsellor-cousin of the five Pāṇḍava brothers, and his violent death. In the *Bhagavadgītā*, he teaches a syncretic religion of devotion to his Pāṇḍava companion Arjuna and reveals him-self to be the all-God, who is called Vishnu.[3] The fusion of Krishna with Vishnu involved a transfer of many of Vishnu's epithets, as well as his functions, to Krishna.[4] The divine-cowherd episodes of Krishna's legend became the focus of the medieval devotional cults that emphasized erotic mysticism, and in the process his divinity became distinct from the other incarnations of Vishnu. Krishna emerged as the supreme god of the Kali Yuga, the cosmic age of darkness.[5]

From ancient times, Indian culture has attributed extraordinary power to names and the act of name-giving, especially the naming of gods. The tra-ditional practice in Hindu ritual of chanting a series of a god's thousand names (*sahasranāmastuti*) is evidence of this. Epithets are characterizing names, frequently taking the form of descriptive compound words (*bahu-vrīhisamāsa*) in Sanskrit. Although some epithets are petrified into obscure ornamental formulas, most of them function to delineate the subject's char-acter by evoking his deeds, relations, physical forms, and qualities.[6] The particular names and epithets a sophisticated poet like Jayadeva chose from among the myriad names of Krishna must have been meant to set the figure in a pattern of specific associations.

Most of Krishna's epithets in the *Gītagovinda* are traceable to older sources. The epithet *Bhagavat*, Lord, which is prominent in the *Mahā-bhārata*, the *Harivaṁśa*, and various Purāṇas and which is referred to in the title of the *Bhagavadgītā*, is notably absent in the *Gītagovinda*. Its ab-sence, along with the absence of terms like *dharma*, *karma*, and *bhakti*, encourages the speculation that Jayadeva was consciously distinguishing the Krishna he worshipped from the object of the orthodox Bhāgavata cult.[7] This is consonant with the poet's concentration on Krishna's special relation to Rādhā, the isolated figure who contrasts with the cowherdess group and who is ignored in early Bhāgavata texts.[8] The epithets *Jagadīśa*, Lord of the World, and *Jayadeva*, God of Triumph, are textually asso-ciated with Krishna for the first time in the *Gītagovinda*. Their use in the opening songs is crucial to appreciating the conceptual framework and movement of the poem. The epithets *Daśavidharūpa* and *Daśākṛtikṛt,* referring to Krishna in his ten incarnations, are similarly significant.

The various epithets are defined below, in order of their appearance in the text of the poem, with references to other sources. Chapters and verses in the text of the *Gītagovinda* are referred to by Roman and Arabic numerals; an asterisk placed after a verse number indicates a refrain.

MĀDHAVA (I.1; III.2; IV.1, 2*, 7; V.7; VII.12, 39; VIII.2*; IX.2*; XI.14*) literally means "related to *madhu.*" *Madhu* may mean "springtime," or "honey," or "the progenitor of Krishna's own Yadu clan." The relation of the progenitor Madhu to the demon Madhu whom Krishna destroys is unclear. Daniel H. H. Ingalls suggests that the whole myth of the demon rests on a misunderstanding of the name Mādhava, "springtime." [9] It may be that the "misunderstanding" was intended by storytellers to amplify the meaning of the epithet as it applies to Krishna. In the *Gītagovinda, madhu* is used to mean "honey" (I.36; VI.2; VII.6; X.2*; XI.18), "springtime" (I.46), and "the demon Madhu" (I.20). The epithets *Madhusūdana,* "killer of Madhu" (I.25, 40; II.17; VII.9), *Madhuripu,* "enemy of Madhu" (II.9, 18; V.1, 14; VI.5; VII.13, 29; XII.9), and *Madhumathana,* "tormentor of Madhu" (XI.2*) indicate that Krishna conquered *madhu,* but it remains uncertain how *madhu* is to be understood. If these epithets and *Mādhava* are understood as a complex of related meanings, they seem to suggest that Krishna conquered and absorbed into himself the power of what he conquered, whether it was "springtime" or "honey" or Krishna's own progenitor, all of which are potentially dangerous and so "demonical." Springtime, personified in Indian literature as the companion of the god of love, is erotically powerful and painful for parted lovers. Honey, the prized raw food of the forest, is cited as an aphrodisiac of power and danger in early brahmanical literature. [10] Lévi-Strauss offers an analysis of honey in South American myths as a paradisaical seducer and disrupter of marital ties, [11] and one can see a parallel relation between Krishna's seductive, antinomian sexual behavior and his metaphoric association with honey. The conventional Indian sexual image of the bee acting like a lover in producing and drinking honey further widens the meaning of Krishna's association with honey. Bees are referred to in the poem by the common Sanskrit epithets *madhukara,* "honey-maker" (I.27; VII.25), *madhupa,* "honey-drinker" (I.36; V.4; XI.4, 18), and *madhuvrata,* "busy with honey" (II.1). The dominant meanings of *madhu* thus provide a strongly erotic context for the verbal play of *Mādhava* and related epithets in the *Gītagovinda*.[12]

vāsudeva (I.2) refers to Krishna's royal birth in the Yadu clan as the son of Vasudeva and Devakī. It is a common epithet of Krishna throughout epic literature.[13]

hari (I.4, 5*, 17*, 27*, 34, 38*, 39, 43, 46; II.1, 2*; IV.9, 17; V.14, 15; VI.2*, 6, 7; VII.3, 7, 10, 14, 29, 38; IX.1, 2, 4, 6, 8, 9; XI.6, 8, 9, 13, 24*, 31; XII.1, 19) literally means "the tawny one," but Vaishnava commentators interpret it to mean "the destroyer of pain," derived from the Sanskrit root √ *hṛ*. Hari is a common name of Vishnu in his cosmic form and his various incarnations in the epics and Purāṇas. It is probably borrowed from the Vedic name of Indra, whose characteristics Vishnu and Krishna absorb.[14] The ambiguity of reference in the name *Hari* reflects the identification of Krishna, as *Jagadīśa*, with the cosmic form and function of Vishnu.[15] The similarity between *Hari* and Śiva's name *Hara*, "the destroyer" (III.11), is exploited by Jayadeva for ironical effect.

keśava (I.5*, 45; IV.11*; VIII.2*; XI.1) means "long-haired." It is traditionally related to Krishna's killing of the horse-demon Keśin.[16] Like *Hari*, it refers ambiguously to Vishnu and Krishna in epic and Purāṇic literature.

jagadīśa (I.5*) means "Lord of the World." In the refrain of the song of invocation, it indicates Krishna's cosmic supremacy. In the Jagannātha cult of Orissa, which probably provided the context for the composition of the *Gītagovinda*, Krishna is identified with the composite Buddhist-Śaivite-Vaishnavite form of Jagannātha.[17]

daśavidharūpa (I.15) means "having a tenfold form." It indicates that Krishna is at once all of the ten forms of cosmic power he assumes in his awesome aspect (*aiśvarya*) in order to save the world. The same is meant by *Daśākṛtikṛt* (I.16). The ten forms of *Jagadīśa* are a variant of the ten incarnations of Vishnu; in Purāṇic literature Krishna instead of Balarāma is usually the eighth incarnation. The incarnations were originally independent legends that came to center on Vishnu as the preserver of order when it is imperiled. Various aspects of the legends are emphasized in different texts. The content of the *Gītagovinda* song is not traceable to any single source.[18]

The awesome aspect of Krishna, which the ten forms vividly portray, recedes as Krishna's lover-hero role (*nāyaka*) is elaborated in the poem to dramatize his honey aspect (*mādhurya*) in relation to Rādhā. But the cosmic power remains a background for the intimacy of the lovers throughout the poem; the intimacy offers a dimension of cosmic power on which human perception can focus. The complex and powerful manifestations of cosmic reality are concentrated in emotions that are carefully patterned for esthetic experience.[19] In the terminology of Indian esthetics, the song of invocation to Krishna's tenfold form expresses the mood of wonder (*adbhutarasa*), whose presence is essential to Jayadeva's religious transformation of the mood of erotic love (*śṛṅgārarasa*).[20]

Jayadeva presents the ten forms of *Jagadīśa* as follows:

1. MĪNAŚARĪRA (I.5), the Fish-form, more commonly called *Matsyāvatāra*. The ancient myth of the deluge and man's rescue by a giant fish, which is told in the *Śatapatha Brāhmaṇa* (I.8.1–6), is the basis of later versions. The *Gītagovinda* refers to the theft of the Vedas from Brahmā by a sea demon as the former is entering the sleep of cosmic dissolution. Hari takes on the form of a fish and, by means of the deluge, destroys the demon and recovers the Vedas.[21]

2. KACCHAPARŪPA (I.6), the Tortoise-form. The *Gītagovinda* refers to the creative power of the giant tortoise in relation to earth, an association that is made in the *Śatapatha Brāhmaṇa* (VII.5.1.5). This form is better known, as *Kūrmāvatāra,* for supporting Mt. Mandara when the gods and demons churn the sea to obtain the elixir of immortality.[22]

3. ŚŪKARARŪPA (I.7), the Boar-form, another name for *Varāhāvatāra*. The giant boar rescues the earth by raising it out of the ocean depths on one of his tusks.[23]

4. NARAHARIRŪPA (I.8), the Man-lion form, another name for *Narasiṁhāvatāra*. It is the form in which Hari destroys the infidel King Hiraṇyakaśipu, who threatened his own son Prahlāda with death because of the son's devotion to Hari. Hiraṇyakaśipu had been given a boon of invulnerability by day or night, by god, man, or beast, inside or outside his palace, and to overcome it the god appears at twilight as a man-lion inside a pillar and reaches out to dismember the king.[24]

5. VĀMANARŪPA (I.9), the Dwarf-form. The three cosmic strides of Vishnu form the basis of the dwarf myth.[25] The demon Bali, usurper of Indra's power, grants three paces of land to Hari when he comes to him in the guise of a dwarf. Then Hari assumes his cosmic shape

averses earth, atmosphere, and heaven. The *Gītagovinda* re-Hari's wet feet, which the demon, in his hospitality, has to welcome his guest.[26]

6. BHṚGUPATIRŪPA (I.10), the form of the Bhṛgu chief better known as *Paraśurāma,* "axe-wielding Rāma," who reestablishes order in the world by putting an end to the tyranny of the warrior class.[27]

7. RĀMAŚARĪRA (I.11), the form of the "charming" Rāmacandra, Prince of Ayodhyā, who is alternately called *Raghupatirūpa.* He is the hero of Vālmīki's epic *Rāmāyaṇa* and of the *Rāmopākhyāna* of the *Mahābhārata* (III.258–76). His purpose as an incarnation of Hari is the killing of the ten-headed demon king Rāvaṇa, whose evil power threatens the world. The abduction of his wife Sītā by Rāvaṇa and his defeat of Rāvaṇa and Rāvaṇa's general Dūṣāṇa, "the corrupting one," are referred to in the second song of the *Gītagovinda* (I.16, 22).[28]

8. HALADHARARŪPA (I.12), the form of the plowman Balarāma, elder brother of Krishna. *Haladharasodara,* "brother of Haladhara," refers directly to Krishna (VII.28). Balarāma and Krishna are alternative incarnations of Vishnu in some texts; in other texts they are both partial incarnations, each representing a hair of Vishnu, one white and one black.[29] Balarāma is known for his addiction to wine, paralleling Krishna's addiction to women. The *Gītagovinda* refers to the episode where he drunkenly orders the Jumna river to move close so he can sport there. When the river fails to obey, he throws his weapon, the plowshare, into her and makes the river bend to him.[30]

9. BUDDHAŚARĪRA (I.13), the form of "the enlightened one," Gautama Buddha. Buddha is not an incarnation in the *Mahābhārata* or the *Harivaṁśa,* but he appears as such in the texts of early Purāṇic literature.[31] The orthodox Hindu view stresses that Buddha's emphasis on moral values, as opposed to Vedic ritual, is valuable only in confusing men and fostering the social chaos that marks the decline of the Kali Yuga. Jayadeva's linking of Buddha's condemnation of Vedic ritual with his compassion for animal victims is a more positive view, consonant with the syncretism characterizing the worship of Krishna as *Jagadīśa* in the *Gītagovinda.*[32]

10. KALKIŚARĪRA (I.14), the form of the avenger, Kalki, who appears with a blazing sword on a white horse at the end of the Kali Yuga to punish barbarians and sinners.[33]

KRṢṆA is anglicized as *Krishna* in this volume to render recurring reference to the hero of the *Gītagovinda* less artificial for English readers (I.16, 26; II.10; VIII.3, 7; X.5; XII.21); it literally means "black," or "dark." It is a prominent name of the epic hero who is identified with Vishnu in the *Mahābhārata* and who is counted as one of the standard incarnations of Vishnu. Kṛṣṇa Devakīputra is mentioned in the *Chāndogya Upaniṣad* (III.17.6) as a pupil of the mythical teacher Ghora Aṅgiras; scholars have made much of the reference, but it is too isolated to be significant. In the *Gītagovinda*, Krishna is *Jagadīśa*, the cosmic power of the Dark Age. His relationship with Rādhā is set in the context of his youthful adventures among the cowherds and his adolescent erotic play with the cowherdesses in Brindaban forest.[34]

JAYADEVA (I.17*) is interpreted as a dependent compound (*tatpuruṣasamāsa*) meaning "God of Triumph." This is derived by reading the refrain of the second song as *jaya jayadeva hare,* "Triumph, God of Triumph, Hari!" to parallel the refrain of the first song, which is *jaya jagadīśa hare,* "Triumph, Lord of the World, Hari!" [35] The commentator Śaṅkaramiśra, referring to the opening verse of the poem, points out that Krishna's triumph as the hero (*nāyaka*) of the *Gītagovinda* is in sexual play (*keli*). Rādhā is called "Love's living goddess of triumph," *anaṅgajayajaṅgama-devatā* (III.15). The epithet of Krishna is identical with the name of the author of the *Gītagovinda*. In this function, *Jayadeva* occurs in the signature stanza (*bhaṇita*) of each song, as well as in some verses (I.2, 4, 15, 24, 34, 45; II.9, 18; III.10; IV.9, 18; V.6, 15; VI.9; VII.10, 20, 29, 38; VIII.9; IX.9; X.9; XI.9, 21, 31; XII.9, 19, 21, 22).[36]

HAṀSA, (I.18), the Indian wild goose, which migrates to the Himalayas every spring to mate on Lake Mānasa, according to legend. It is symbolic of the Universal Spirit (*parabrahman*). *Mānasa* also means "mental" and the poet's reference is to Krishna as the Universal Spirit in the minds of sages.

MURĀRI (I.37; V.12; VII.21, 22*; XI.21), or *Muravairin* (X.9), means "enemy of Mura." Mura is a demon who is associated with another demon named Naraka in the *Mahābhārata* (I.59, etc.), as in the *Gītagovinda* (I.20).[37]

PĪTAVASANA (I.38; II.7), or *Pītāmbara* (XII.20), means "wearing a yellow cloth." It is an ancient epithet of Krishna, referring to the light garment that contrasts with his dark skin.[38]

VANAMĀLIN (I.38; V.2*, 8*; VII.31*) means "wearing a garland of forest flowers" and symbolizes Krishna's sensual presence in the forest.[39]

GOVINDA (II.19; V.17; VI.1; XI.23; XII.21) is probably a Prākritic form of *gopendra* (*gov' inda*), which means "chief of the cowherds." It can also be derived from *go* √*vid* to mean "protector of cows."[40] In either case, the epithet refers to Krishna's adolescence in the forest among the pastoral people of Vraja, the period of his awesome feats of strength, seductive flute playing, and sexual rites. The title *Gītagovinda* has these associations; the young dark lord of the forest is the subject of the poet's singing.

KEŚIMATHANA (II.11*) means "tormentor of the demon Keśin." In the *Harivaṁśa* (62.69), Keśin is called "the meanest of horses," *turagādhama*.[41]

KAṀSĀRI (III.1) means "enemy of Kaṁsa." It refers to the rivalry between Krishna and his uncle, the demonic King Kaṁsa.[42]

UPENDRA (IV.20) means "Indra's younger brother."[43] In the *Gītagovinda* verse it is used to form a pun on the name of the meter *upendravajrā*.

JANĀRDANA (VII.12) means "exciting to men." It is a common epithet of Krishna in the *Mahābhārata*, the *Harivaṁśa*, and the *Bhāgavata Purāṇa*.

NĀRĀYAṆA (XII.2*) literally means "related to *nara*, man." In the *Śatapatha Brāhmaṇa* (XIII.3.4.1) it is an epithet of Puruṣa, the primordial man. Throughout the *Mahābhārata* it is the name of Vishnu or Krishna in the role of cosmic creator.[44]

YADUNANDANA (XII.12, 12*) means "joy of the Yadu clan." Like the epithet *Vāsudeva*, it refers to Krishna's royal birth.

In addition to the epithets that Jayadeva chose to characterize Krishna, references to characters, places, and events from various Vaishnava myths are used to expand the context of the poem. The role of Krishna's foster-father, the cowherd-chief Nanda, in the opening verse is barely indicated by the adverbial compound *nandanideśatah*, "at Nanda's order." But the presence of the name emphasizes that Krishna is young as his sexual play begins.[45] References to Krishna's defeat of the serpent-king Kāliya (I.19) [46] and the bird-demoness Pūtanikā (VIII.8) [47] evoke heroic events of his legend. Kāliya was punished for befouling the Jumna waters and Pūtanikā was killed when the baby Krishna sucked her life from her by taking the poisoned breast she offered him. Garuḍa (I.20) is the anthropomorphized eagle who usually serves as Vishnu's vehicle.[48] The sexual freedom enjoyed by the adolescent cowherd is symbolized by Krishna's simple bamboo flute, which is called *vaṁśa* (I.43; II.2, 19) or *veṇu* (V.9).[49] Like the flower arrows shot by the god of love, Krishna's magical flute is an adolescent instrument for arousing and sustaining sexual desire. Both the arrow and the flute, with their obvious phallic significance, function in this way in the myths of many societies.[50] The culminating effect of Krishna's flute-playing is the ritual circular dance, called *rāsa* (I.43; II.2*), which he performs under the full moon of autumn with the cowherdesses. The common version of the story recounts Krishna's seduction of the cowherdesses by the melodious call of his flute in the woods of Brindaban (*Vṛndāvana*) on the banks of the river Jumna (*Yamunā*).[51] Krishna remains elusive, but promises to dance with the girls in autumn, when the heat and rains are finished. On a night of the full moon, Krishna goes toward the forest playing his flute. The cowherdesses follow and form a circle around him, like stars around the moon. By his magic power, he multiplies himself to dance with all the cowherdesses at once.[52] This rite of autumn acts as a foil for his springtime play with his cowherdess consort Rādhā.

In Indian myth, spring is the ally of Kāma, the god of love. The sexual aggression of Love is portrayed in the myth of his body's destruction by Śiva when he interrupted Śiva's meditation with flower arrows to arouse the divine ascetic's desire for Pārvatī, the daughter of Himālaya. In his relation to Rādhā, Krishna is both the object of Love's attack and the embodiment of Love's creative sensuality.[53]

By representing his divine hero with a complex of characteristics known from older religious sources, Jayadeva thus sets Krishna's relation with Rādhā in a sacred framework. Krishna's relation to all living beings is expressed through his ten incarnate forms. His personal spiritual relation to human beings is expressed through the form of the flute-playing adolescent cowherd. His intense spiritual intimacy with an individual human being is expressed through the divine sensuality of his love with Rādhā.

As the divine lover and object of the poet's worship, Krishna is the embodiment of erotic mood (*śṛṅgāramūrtiman*, I.46) and the essence of esthetic experience (*ekarasa*, XI.24*). His relation with Rādhā epitomizes the classical pattern of erotic love in Sanskrit drama and poetry. Krishna is referred to by standard forms of address given for the dramatic hero (*nāyaka*) in Bharata's *Nāṭyaśāstra*, such as "beloved" or "lover" (*kānta*, VII.11, XII.10, 11; *dayita*, I.41, VII.17, 30; *priya*, IV.21, V.16, VII.30, VIII.1, X.12, XI.32, 33, XII.5, 13; *vallabha*, VII.30),[54] "cheat" (*kitava*, VI.10),[55] and "rogue" (*śaṭha*, VII.30).[56] These familiar forms of address complement the sensuous surface that emerges from descriptions of Krishna's ornamented physical presence and his manifestations of emotion. By such means the poet encourages his audience to approach the divine lover through esthetic experience. The ingenious integration of religious, erotic, and esthetic meaning that Jayadeva achieves in the structure of the *Gītagovinda* is basic in the character of Krishna too.

5 Rādhā: Consort of Krishna's Springtime Passion

Rādhā is one of the most obscure figures in early Indian literature. Until Jayadeva made her the heroine of his poem, she appeared only in stray verses scattered through various Purāṇas, anthologies of Prākrit and Sanskrit poetry, works of literary esthetics, grammar, poetry, drama, and a few inscriptions. In the *Gītagovinda,* Rādhā is neither a wife nor a worshipping rustic playmate. She is an intense, solitary, proud female who complements and reflects the mood of Krishna's passion. She is Krishna's partner in a secret and exclusive love, contrasted in the poem with the circular *rāsa* dance Krishna performs with the entire group of cowherdesses. Krishna disappears after this dance, deserting the cowherdesses; but he stays with Rādhā to admire and ornament her. Her relationship with Krishna culminates in their union and mutual "victory" (*jaya*) over each other. In Jayadeva's view, the profound intimacy of Krishna's concentration on Rādhā, in contrast with the diffusion of erotic energy in his play with the cowherdesses, is the perfection of Krishna's nature.[1]

Jayadeva's reference to his heroine focuses on one name, *Rādhā* (I.1, 26; II.1; III.1; IV.20; V.1; VI.2*; XI.1, 13, 14*, 24, 32; XII.1, XII.11) and its diminutive, *Rādhikā* (I.37; III.2; IV.1, 11*; X.9, XI.2*; XII.2*). Names of Krishna's divine consort, such as *Śrī* (I.2; I.23), *Padmāvatī* (I.2; X.9; XI.21), *Kamalā* (I.17), *Padmā* (I.25), and *Lakṣmī* (XI.22), occur to place Rādhā in the appropriate cosmic context. Rādha's role as the female counterpart of her lover is consonant with the meaning of her name, which is related to the word *rādhas*. In Vedic and Purāṇic literature, *rādhas* and other forms of the root √*rādh* have meaning of "perfection" and "success," even "wealth."[2] The Vedic god most closely associated with *rādhas* is Indra, who bears the epithet "Lord of Success" (*rādhaspati*).[3] In the *Mahābhārata* and various Purāṇas, the rivalry between Indra and Vishnu/Krishna results in the transference of elements of Indra's great power to Vishnu/Krishna. Among these elements are female powers associated with Indra, such as Śrī in the episode of the churning of the ocean.[4] Indra lost Śrī through a curse by the sage Durvāsa and Vishnu reclaimed her as his spouse. A similar pattern may well account for Krishna's role as "Lord of Success" (*rādhaspati*) in relation to *Rādhā,* the feminine personification of *rādhas.* This explanation helps to clarify the parallelism between the pair Śrī/Lakṣmī-Vishnu/Krishna and the pair Rādhā-Krishna that is suggested in many stray verses antedating the *Gītagovinda.* There is no need to construct fanciful etymologies for the word *rādhā,* but this has been the approach of the Sanskrit commentators on the *Gītagovinda* and more recently of the linguist Sukumar Sen.[5] Such accounts offer no clue to why the association between Rādhā and Krishna was made.

In the absence of direct textual evidence it remains impossible to know when and in what circumstances the Rādhā-Krishna pair originated. What we find in the available Prākrit and Sanskrit sources suggests that the poets and critics are dealing with a familiar subject. The name Rādhā seems to carry overtones of meaning from astral mythology. Although there is no reference to the pair in Vedic literature, the word *rādhā* occurs in the *Atharva Veda* (XIX.7.3) in relation to the two stars called *viśākhā.*[6] Later references to *rādhā* as the name of a feminine constellation or star-cluster (*nakṣatrā*) associate her with Indra. Indra is called a "cowherd" (*gopā*) and is paired with a *viśākhā* in several Vedic contexts. In the *Taittirīya Brāhmaṇa* (3.1.1.11)[7] two *viśākhās* are described as the chief female consorts (*adhipatnī*) of the male constellations (*nakṣatra*) and are paired with Indra and Agni, who are called the two best cowherds. In the *Taittirīya Samhitā* (4.4.11),[8] in the section where the building of the fire altar (*agnicayana*) is described, the layers of bricks are pairs of feminine constellations and masculine deities. The feminine *viśākhās* are paired with the masculine deities Indra and Agni. These associations are especially significant when it is recalled that Indra is the "Lord of Success" (*rādhaspati*).

In the same *Taittirīya Samhitā* passage the pairs of months of the various seasons are named; the months of spring (*vāsantikāv ṛtū*) are named *madhu* and *mādhava.* In the *Mahābhārata,* Vishnu is related to the constellations by his epithet *Nakṣatrin,* "Lord of Constellations," and to spring by the epithets *Mādhu* and *Mādhava* that he shares with Krishna.[9] *Mādhava* is a major epithet of Krishna in epic and later literature. Krishna is also associated in several contexts with various feminine constellations.[10] Whether or not the equation of *rādhā* with *viśākhā* in commentaries on the *Atharva Veda* passage is based on a "misunderstanding" of the word *anurādhā,* as Whitney suggests, it is clear that by the fifth century, *rādhā* was held to be another name for the constellation *viśākhā.*[11] With the equating of month names and constellation names, *viśākhā* became one of the months of spring, creating another link between *rādhā* and *mādhava.* The somewhat esoteric character of these associations may have increased the appeal of Rādhā as a consort for Krishna in a secret relationship. In these two aspects, she represents, like Lakṣmī, the power of "success" and she incarnates, like Śiva's Pārvatī, a phenomenon of nature. Both aspects illuminate her association with Krishna.[12]

Because of the fluidity of Purāṇic texts, it is impossible to date or locate the relationship of Rādhā and Krishna from them. However, the pattern of Rādhā's presence and absence in some major Purāṇas is relevant to the problem. As disciples of the sixteenth-century Vaishnava saint Caitanya, who was considered an incarnation of the divine lovers Rādhā and Krishna, the Gosvāmins searched Purāṇic literature to find references that would establish Rādhā's old and high status within orthodox Vaishnavism.[13] References to Rādhā by name in early Purāṇas such as the *Matsya,* the *Linga,* and the *Varāha* are significant, but few. Rādhā's elaborate treatment in the *Brahmavaivarta* and *Padma* Purāṇas seems to postdate the Caitanya movement.[14] There is no direct reference to Rādhā in the *Harivaṁśa,* the *Viṣṇu Purāṇa* or the *Bhāgavata Purāṇa.* But the mention of a favored cowherdess who is "worshipped" or "desired" (*ārādhitā*) by Krishna in the tenth book of the *Bhāgavata Purāṇa*[15] led the Gosvāmins to derive the name Rādhā from *ārādhitā* and to claim Rādhā's place in the text.[16]

The heroine of the *Gītagovinda* is so complex that it seems absurd to seek Jayadeva's model for her in the allusions to the arrogant girl (*dṛptā*) of the *Bhāgavata* episode. Krishna's special mistress is presented there to criticize the exclusivism that Krishna's relationship with her represents. If the *Bhāgavata* authors are referring to Krishna's consort Rādhā, they seem to be rejecting her relationship with Krishna as an inappropriate model for the devotee. The possessive attitude manifested in her secret encounter with Krishna is antithetical to the values presented in the *Bhāgavata* and the attitude is criticized for its perversity (*daurātmya,* X.30.42). It is not unlikely that the authors of the *Bhāgavata* knew a rival cult centering on Krishna and his cowherdess-consort and were critical of it.

Charlotte Vaudeville, in her article entitled "Evolution of Love-

Symbolism in Bhagavatism,"[17] has stated her supposition that the author of the *Bhāgavata* was specifically rejecting the figure of Nappiṇṇai, as she appears in the Tamil Āḻvār poetry of Āṇḍāl and Nāmmāḻvār. Here Nappiṇṇai is the daughter, or daughter-in-law, of Nandagopāl and the wife of Krishna; she is an incarnation of Vishnu's consort Nīladevī.[18] It is possible that Nappiṇṇai is the source of the Rādhā conception in Prākrit and Sanskrit literature, but the two figures more likely represent independent variants; their characteristic relations with Krishna are different. In the ritual dance called *kuravai,* Krishna dances with his wife Nappiṇṇai, while Krishna's relationship with Rādhā is a secret, erotic rite.[19]

The character of Rādhā and her unique association with Krishna that Jayadeva brought to his *Gītagovinda* from earlier literature is not apparent from any single source, but details emerge from the collection of stray verses that refer to her. A chronological catalogue of these references suggest an old tradition surrounding the secret love of Rādhā and Krishna.[20]

From the *Sattasaī* of Hāla (dated first to seventh centuries by various scholars) :[21]

> Krishna, removing cow-dust from Rādhikā
> With the breath of your mouth,
> You sweep away the high esteem
> These other cowherdesses have for you. (86)

From the *Gaüḍavaho* of Vākpati (late seventh or early eighth century) :[22]

> Let nailmarks Rādhā makes remove your pain—
> They are rich with mood.
> They are shining on Krishna's chest
> Like his magical kaustubha gem. (22)

From the *Veṇīsaṃhāra* of Bhaṭṭa Nārāyaṇa (antedates A.D. 800) :[23]

> Angered in sensual play, she lost her mood for love
> In the rāsa dance on sandbanks of the Jumna river.
> When Kaṃsa's foe followed Rādhikā
> As she left in a choking veil of tears,
> His body hairs seemed to bristle
> From his steps touching her footprints
> And from her calmed, loving looks—
> May you prosper from Krishna's innocent plea! (2)

From the *Dhvanyāloka* of Ānandavardhana (mid-ninth century) : [24]

Say, friend, if all is well still with the bowers
that grow upon the Jumna bank,
companions to the dalliance of cowherd girls
. and witnesses to Rādhā's love.
Now that there is no use to cut their fronds
to make them into beds for love,
I fear their greenness will have faded
and they grown old and hard. (2.6)

Gracious love, Rādhā is difficult indeed to please—
Her tears fall even as you wipe them away
With the cloth that covered some true love's loins.
"Women's hearts are hard, so enough flattery! Leave me alone!"
He was told this whenever Hari tried to placate her—
May he grant you his blessing! (3.41)

From the *Dhvanyālokalocana* of Abhinavagupta (early tenth century) :[25]

Then when demon Madhu's foe had gone to Dvāravatī,
Rādhā embraced a sweet vine growing on the Jumna bank,
A little bent from the way he made it quiver—
Rādhā's lamenting
In a faltering voice choked by heavy tears
Made even the waterbirds wail regretfully.

From the *Kāvyamimāṁsa* of Rājaśekhara (late ninth or early tenth century), as an illustration of the poetic figure *tulyadehitulya*, an imitation that resembles the similarity between two similar persons:[26]

Then we are going to give the different types of the imitation *tulyadehitulya*. . . . the change of subjects gives a different shape to the same theme: this is the change of subject.

May the winds of Śiva's sighs protect you
As they arise from the hollow of his right nostril,
Making lines in the ash-dust on his body,
Disrupting his yogic breathing exercise,
Licked by the serpent sheltered in his ear,
Stealing coolness the moon gives,
Witnessing the agony his mind suffers
When his body is parted from angry Pārvatī.

May Hari's sighs protect you
As they burn from the fire deep within,

Boiling the lotus-honey from his navel,
Wilting the garland on his breast,
Drunk in and spit out because of their heat
By the trembling serpent who forms his couch,
Witnessing his memory of Rādhā's love,
And heard jealously by goddess Śrī.

The occurrence of Rādhā's name in the two oldest-known Sanskrit compositions in mixed prose and verse (*campū-kāvya*) is significant. But the name occurs only once in the *Damayantīkathā* (early tenth century), and once in the *Yaśastilakacampūkāvya* (A.D. 959) and the passages are spare in detail relating to Rādhā.[27] In the *Damayantīkathā* passage the name Rādhā is part of an elaborate pun. The *Yaśastilaka* reference simply says, "Thus indeed—formerly, did Gaṅgā not sport with Maheśvara, Rādhā with Nārāyaṇa, Bṛhaspati's wife with the Moon, Tārā with Valin?"

From inscriptions (dated A.D. 974, 982, and 986) of Vākpati-Muñja, a Paramāra ruler of Malwa, in which the same two verses open each inscription, one in praise in Śiva as the lord of Pārvatī and this one in praise of Krishna as the deserted lover (*virahin*) of Rādhā:[28]

May the active body of demon Mura's enemy protect you!
Lakṣmī's face could not please it, the ocean's waters could not cool it,
The lotus in the lake of his own navel was powerless to pacify it,
Fragrant breath from serpent Śeṣa's thousand mouths could not soothe it—
It was so sick with the pain of Rādhā's desertion.

From the *Sarasvatīkaṇṭhābharaṇa* of Bhoja (ca. A.D. 1000–55)[29] is a verse (2.294) that is an exercise in word play known as *kavināmāṅkāṣṭa-pattrabandha*. Here the poet's name, Rājaśekhara, is hidden in a poem in palindromes and puns; the name emerges through a diagram of an eight-petaled lotus. The diagram was executed by H. S. Phāṭak of the Mysore Oriental Research Institute. The verse can be paraphrased roughly as follows: "She who bestowed a kingdom of defects, a knower of *rasa* that gives expansion ($\sqrt{ra}$), who speaks pretentious speech, who does wrong to the world, the full-moon maiden, whose eyelashes are like serpent Śeṣa, whose eye leads to *nītiśāstra,* she who travels in the sky, whose love is praiseworthy, who is charming, whose penance is several, carrier of the moon, Śrī, whose sword is sharp—let Rādhā protect me; she is the incarnation who brings down serpent knowledge for masters of will who have their egos centered in Śiva." Also, from the same text:

राजशेखरकमलबन्धः

"Are you comfortable, Rādhā?" "Are you happy, Kaṁsa?"
"Kaṁsa?" "What is the difference between Kaṁsa and Rādhā?"
With these retorts of the cowherdess Pārī,
Hari triumphs in self-conscious laughter. (2.351)

As he tries repeatedly to lift
The raincloud-dark reflection of his own bright form,
Mistaking it for the black border of a garment
On the golden globe of Rādhā's breast,
Hari triumphs,
Laughing in shame as his love laughs at him. (3.110)

You left the house for the river to fetch water—you do not return.
Saying, "I shall bathe," you stop at bowers of vines on the Jumna bank.
Tethering the cows, you enter the thick woods of Mt. Govardhana.
Rādhā, didn't you catch sight of Krishna, Devakī's son? (4.177)

May the god who gracefully toys with Rādhā's cloth
On the surface of her breasts protect you!
Hari's hand is trembling
With sudden fear at their first encounter. (5.235)

"I have recently left Gokula, and the thought of Rādhā
Confounds me out of sleep—let it leave my bed and let 'Rādhā'
Stop coming in place of other names by day! I am afraid of this!"
May Hari's fatigue protect you!
He is spending sleepless nights, repeating Lakṣmī's name alone by day,
Trying to forget Rādhā, and delighting goddess Śrī. (5.448)

Seeing how thin Hari's arms were as he carelessly lifted Mt. Govardhana,
She rested her hand on Hari's shoulder and placed her feet on his,
Wanting to help him lift the mountain that was out of her reach—
Let the empty motions of Rādhā's hands in the sky triumph forever! (5.493)

From the *Daśāvatāracarita* of Kṣemendra (composed in A.D. 1066):[30]

While Krishna was kissing swarms of glowing nubile women,
Rādhā became most beloved for his joy—like jasmine for a bee. (83)

Then in the morning, having mounted the armed chariot,
Akrūra, Balarāma, and Krishna went to Mathurā with their retinue. (169)
"How could I have come here without bidding farewell to Rādhā?"
Mādhava sighed, felt discontent, languid, anxious at leaving. (170)
Going by way of hidden places in secret thickets of Gokula,
Krishna looked longingly, his face turned back,
The border of his garment held by his friend the forest earth—
He recalled Rādhā's "No! No! No!" while he loosened her skirt knot,

Her syllables marked by her confusion,
Her body wondrous in fear of love, her words barely intelligible. (171)
Filled with fire of Krishna's desertion when he left for Kamsa's city,
Like antelopes lying on smooth green banks in secret coves of the Godāvarī,
Secretly, in Gokula grass, cowherdesses passionately sang Krishna's virtues,
Heard by herds of cows standing ruminating, ears intimately erect. (172)
"His love is new and graced by shining youth,
Seductive to young women in the easy play of its gentle enchantment;
He subjugates the family of serpent Kāliya in turbulent Jumna waters,
Black as swarms of bees, cuckoos, dark lotuses, and kohl;
He is harsh in killing great demons like Keśi and his sons,
Tearing dangers from Gokula, upholding Mt. Govardhana—
Could anyone's eyes help drowning in him when he is addicted to passion,
A trembling wave of love, delighting delightful young women?" (173)
While each virtue in Krishna's ocean of virtues
Was sung with passionate feeling,
Passion rose secretly in the cowherd girls
And frenzy struck them again and again. (174)
Since Krishna had gone away without speaking
In his zeal to show deference in the presence of the elders,
Doe-eyed women who carelessly slept on cool ground under bakula trees,
When they met him in dream embraces,
Made their slender creeper bodies echo their words by writhing—
"Rogue, let go! Let go, cheat!" the young women loudly cried. (175)
With tears, flowing away like life in Mādhava's desertion,
Falling on her breasts' firm tips, Rādhā was like a laden kadamba tree
As tears were strewn by her endless sighing and trembling gait—
Darkened by the delusion that was bound to all her hopes,
She became like the new rainy season engulfed in darkness. (176)

From the *Subhāṣitaratnakoṣa* compiled by Vidyākara (latter half of eleventh century);[31] these three references have not been noted in earlier works:

"O Lakṣmaṇa, these clouds distress me who have lost my Sītā.
The cruel kadamba-scented breezes cut me to the quick."
So speaking, in his sleep, of separation
suffered in a former birth, may Hari,
glanced at jealously by Rādhā, bring you joy. (131)

"Go on ahead, milkmaids, taking home the pots already full.
Rādhā will follow later when the older cows are milked."
May Krishna, who by subterfuge thus made the cattle station

deserted but for Rādhā and for him,
the god, foster-son of Nanda,
steal away your ills.   (139)

The pilgrims in the street have warded off the painful cold
with their broad quilts sewn of a hundred rags;
and now with voices clear and sweet
'they break the morning slumber of the city folk
with songs of the secret love of Mādhava and Rādhā.   (980)

From the *Vikramānkadevacarita* of Bilhaṇa (late eleventh century):[32]

Let Krishna's sword, "Delighter," reflecting joyful Lakṣmī
In its blade, hold out intense joy for you—
For demon Mura's enemy it perpetually revives
The memory of graceful Rādhā in the Jumna river's flow.   (I.5)

[On his journey southward from Kashmir, Bilhaṇa stops at Brindaban.]

Broken by Rādhā's broad hips, which sway as she swings them,
Even now the trees in Krishna's playground have not recovered—
When the circle of Mathurā's sages was shaken by playful banter,
The poet spent several days in wandering around Brindaban.   (XVIII.87)

From the *Siddhahemaśabdānuśāna* of Hemacandra (A.D. 1088–1172):[33]

Hari danced in the courtyard; the world was wonder-struck.
Let the glow of Rādhā's breasts endure!   (4.420.2)

Though Hari sees every person with full regard,
Still his glance goes wherever Rādhā is—
Who can arrest eyes ensnared by love?   (4.422.5)

From the *Naiṣadhīyacarita* of Śrīharṣa (latter half of twelfth century) [34]
is a verse based on the double meaning of the names *Rādhā* and *Śrīvatsa*.
The name *Rādhā* here refers to both Krishna's consort and Karṇa's foster
mother in the *Mahābhārata;* the enemy of Rādhā's son Karṇa is Arjuna.
Śrīvatsa means "Śrī's child" and the curl of hair on the chest of Vishnu
or Krishna.

Rādhā is as dear to you as your life—
Your friendship with Arjuna, foe of Rādhā's son, is unfitting.
But is it fitting for Śrī's lover
To hold "the child of Śrī" on your own heart forever?

From the *Āryasaptaśatī* of Govardhana (late twelfth century):[35]

Friend, Tulasī, garland on the head of Madhu's foe,
Why compare yourself in vain with Rādhā?
All the outpouring of your fragrance
Is just to perfume her feet. (431)

When stories of how his head was washed
In royal ablution are told about Krishna,
Rādhā, her eyes slowed by the weight of pride,
Looks down at the lotus of her own feet. (488)

In order to shame demon Madhu's enemy,
Whose mind was drunk with all the cowherd girls,
Rādhā, feigning innocence, asked for the story of Śiva,
Who was satisfied with half his wife. (508)

Lovely women on shores of the milky sea
Eat balls of milk made thick
By hot winds of Lakṣmī's sighing,
And they sing the praises of Rādhā. (509)

When Krishna is wandering in search
Of Rādhā's impassioned quivering eyes,
The god of love is creating an arrow
Perfected to pierce the ten directions. (530)

To complement Krishna's role as the dramatic hero (*nāyaka*) and the embodiment of erotic mood (*śṛṅgāramūrtiman*), Rādhā is the dramatic heroine (*nāyikā*) and is identified with passion (*rati*), the emotion (*bhāva*) through which erotic mood (*śṛṅgārarasa*) develops. As passion personified, she is also consort to Kāma. When Rādhā fulfills Krishna's passion, she provides the emotional means for a sympathetic audience (*rasikajana*) to enjoy the extraordinary experience of Krishna's springtime love. Through her suffering during Krishna's desertion, as described by her to her friend (*sakhī*) and by her friend to Krishna, she is transformed into a powerful consort, appropriate to share Krishna's divine love.[36]

Rādhā is referred to by the standard forms of address for a dramatic heroine. Among them are "foolish woman" (*mugdhavadhū*, I.38*; *mugdhā* V.17; X.11,12; XI.2*), "fiercely angry woman" (*caṇḍī*, X.11,13; XI.7),[37] "proud woman" (*mānini*, IX.2*), and "emotional woman" (*bhāvini*, XII.6).

Rādhā plays the classical heroine in seven of the eight stylized psychological states of relation to the hero (*nāyikāvasthā*) that are delineated by

theorists of Indian drama.[38] Each of the states is identified in the text
Jayadeva with reference to its technical name or to its characteristic si_o...
The increasing intensity of Rādhā's desolation is dramatized by concrete
manifestations of her condition in the various states.[39] The culminating
emotional intensity of her divine love with Krishna is not effected
through psychological depth. It is effected through the accumulation of
sensuous details expressing the chaos of feeling and fantasy a deserted
woman suffers.

After their first night of love, Krishna deserts Rādhā to play with other
cowherdesses. Her demand for Krishna's exclusive love, in the context of
his common love (*sādhāraṇapraṇaya*, II.1) with the other cowherdesses,
generates her state of envy (*īrṣyā*). A deserted cowherdess longing for
love (*utkaṇṭhitagopavadhū*, II.18) is her basic condition throughout the
night of the drama. The power of her longing makes Krishna reciprocate
her love and suffer as much as she does in their separation. The longing is
emotionally amplified by the other states. She waits in vain for Krishna,
dressed and ornamented for love (*vāsakasajjā*, VI.8). She feels herself de-
ceived (*vañcitā*) by her friends (VII.3*) and by Krishna (VIII.7,9).[40] She
is jealously enraged (*khaṇḍitayuvati*, VIII.9), imagining the marks of
love a rival has inflicted on Krishna. She is remorseful after quarreling
(*kalahāntaritā*, IX.1). At her friend's urging, her modesty abandons her
(*salajjā lajjā vyagamad iva*, XI.33) and she goes to meet her lover.[41] After
their ecstatic reunion, she feels her lover in her power (*svādhīnabhartṛkā*,
XII.11). The graceful intimacy of Rādhā's triumph gives Jayadeva's
drama its unique flavor.

The character of Rādhā in the *Gītagovinda* established her as Krishna's
consort within later traditions of the Krishna cult. Her relative obscurity
in earlier literature encouraged the view that Jayadeva had invented
"Rādhā." Although he clearly did not invent her, he did create a unique
heroine for Indian devotional literature.[42]

NOTES

1 Jayadeva: The Wandering Poet

1. There exist other literary works whose authorship is also designated "Jayadeva," but there is no evidence to associate the author of the *Gītagovinda* with any of these works. The play on the life of Rāma, entitled *Prasannarāghava* (edited by S. M. Paranjpe; Poona: Shiralkar, 1894), bears little conceptual or stylistic resemblance to the *Gītagovinda*. It is first quoted in the anthology *Sūktimuktāvalī* of Bhagadatta Jalhaṇa (edited by E. Krishnamacharya, Gaekwad's Oriental Series, 82; Baroda: Central Library, 1938), dated A.D. 1257. The Sikh tradition that lists Jayadeva among the great saints of India is based on the sixteenth century *Bhaktamāl* legend (see note 2 below), but the two mixed Prākrit-Apabhraṁśa verses attributed to him in the *Guru Granth Sahib* are characterized by the kind of abstract devotionalism that is not present in the *Gītagovinda;* see M. A. Macauliffe, *The Sikh Religion* (1909; reprint, New Delhi: S. Chand, 1963), vol. VI, pp. 4–17. Jayadeva the author of the work on prosody entitled *Chandahśāstra* is referred to by the tenth-century critic Abhinavagupta in his *Abhinavabhāratī;* see P. K. Gode, *Studies in Indian Literary History* (Bombay: Bharatiya Vidya Bhavan, 1953), vol. I, pp. 138–43. The one-act Sanskrit drama *Pīyūṣalaharī* is attributed to the author of the *Gītagovinda* on the basis of similarity in content; see K. Kar, "Pīyūṣa-laharī: A One-act Drama of Poet Jayadeva," *Journal of the Kalinga Historical Research Society*, 1956, pp. 291–327. Many other derivative works are attributed to the author of the *Gītagovinda* with no better claim. The author of the *Candrāloka*, a work on poetics, is known as Jayadeva Pīyūṣavarṣa (see text edited by N. S. Khiste, Kashi Sanskrit Series 75; Varanasi: Chowkhamba Sanskrit Series Office, 1929); nothing in the text suggests identical authorship of it and the *Gītagovinda*.

2. The most widely known version of the legendry life of Jayadeva is in the Hindi *Bhaktamāl*, edited and rewritten by Nārāyaṇadāsa in the middle of the seventeenth century from old Hindi verses by Nābhājīdāsa (edited by S. B. Rupakala; Lucknow: Tejkumar Press, 1969), pp. 343–64; see G. Grierson, "Modern Vernacular Hindi Literature," *Journal of the Asiatic Society of Bengal*, 57 (1888), 27. On the Hindi version is based the Sanskrit *Bhaktamālā* of Candradatta; *sargas* 39–41, which give the life of Jayadeva, are quoted in the introduction to the Telang and Panshikar edition of the *Gītagovinda* with the commentaries of Kumbhakarṇa and Śankaramiśra (Bombay: Nirṇayasāgara Press, 1899), pp. 1–19. The best-known Bengali version of the Jayadeva legend is Vanamālīdāsa's *Jayadevacarita* (edited by A. K. Goswami; Calcutta: Vangiya Sahitya Parishad, 1905, B.S. 1312). The legend is also related in the sixteenth-century *Śekhśubhoḍayā*, which centers on the life of a Muslim holy man who visited the court of Lakṣmaṇasena; see Sukumar Sen, ed., *Śekhśubhodayā*, Bibliotheca Indica, no. 286(Calcutta: Asiatic Society, 1963). Aspects of the legend are referred to in all the later commentaries.

A verse that names Jayadeva's parents as Bhojadeva and Rāmādevī is not found in all manuscripts of the *Gītagovinda*, but its presence in the most conservative version of the text justifies its inclusion in the present edition (XII.22). The legendary account of Jayadeva's life identifies Bhojadeva as a brahman of Kanauj who migrated to the village of Kindubilva.

3. S. N. Chatterji, *Jayadeva, Makers of Indian Literature* (New Delhi: Sahitya

1 Jayadeva: The Wandering Poet (cont.)

Akademi, 1973); this is largely based on the material of Harekrishna Mukhopādhyāya that introduces his edition of the Bengali version of the *Gitagovinda*, with the commentary of Caitanyadāsa entitled *Bālabodhinī*, in *Kavijayadeva o śrīgītagovinda* (Calcutta: Gurudās Mukhopādhyāy, 1956, B.S. 1362). See also the introduction, in Latin, by C. Lassen to his edition and Latin translation of the *Gitagovinda* (Bonn, 1836); R. Pischel, "Die Hofdichter des Lakṣmaṇasena," *Abhandlungen der Königlichen Gesellschaft der Wissenschaften zu Göttigen*, philol.-histor. Klasse, 39 (1893), 1–39; K. N. Mahapatra, "New Light on Poet Jayadeva, The Author of the *Gitagovinda*," *The Orissa Historical Research Journal*, 7 (1959), 191–207; S. C. Mukherji, *A Study of Vaiṣṇavism in Ancient and Medieval Bengal* (Calcutta: Punthi Pustak, 1966), pp. 91–107; N. K. Sahu, editor, *Souvenir on Srijayadeva* (Bhubaneswar: The Jayadeva Sanskrutika Parishad, 1968), articles by S. N. Rajaguru, N. K. Sahu, and K. N. Mahapatra, pp. 1–41.

Richard and Carol Salomon have reminded me how similar the controversy about Jayadeva's place of origin is to the controversy surrounding the "Old Bengali" *Caryāpada* literature. The two cases suggest that the culture, as well as the language and literature, of eastern India was more or less uniform at this time. See note 13 to section 2 below.

4. See *Saduktikarṇāmṛta*, critical edition, edited by S. C. Banerji (Calcutta: K. L. Mukhopadhyay, 1965), author index, p. 8. For the best available account of the reign of Lakṣmaṇasena, see R. C. Majumdar, *History of Ancient Bengal* (Calcutta: G. Bharadwaj, 1971), pp. 231–50, 254–59.

5. *Skm.* 659 = GG. VI.11; *Skm.* 1144 = GG. XII.10. Three additional verses attributed to Jayadeva in the *Saduktikarṇāmṛta* are found in the text of the *Gitagovinda* on which Kumbhakarṇa commented (see edition of Telang and Panshikar) and which became the popular version after the sixteenth century. However, these are not found in conservative versions of the *Gitagovinda* and are included in the present critical edition only as variants: *Skm.* 294 = GG XI.33†; *Skm.* 1134 = GG XII.23† (a); *Skm.* 1160 = GG XII.23† (c). Many of the remaining verses show thematic and stylistic similarities to the *Gitagovinda* verses, but others attest the poet's ability to compose panegyrics to a king and descriptions of battle; see Chatterji, *Jayadeva*, pp. 20–28, for a collection of these verses.

6. Both Kumbhakarṇa, in whose text this is I.4, and the other early commentator, Mānāṅka (text and commentary edited by V. M. Kulkarni; Ahmedabad: L. D. Bharatiya Sanskriti Vidyamandira, 1965), interpret this verse with reference to Lakṣmaṇasena. Mānāṅka considers the king to be the author of the verse and Kumbhakarṇa considers the five, plus another named Śrutidhara, to be scholars at the court of Lakṣmaṇasena. If Jayadeva composed the verse, he is probably elaborating the preceding reference to the goddess of speech (*vāgdevatā*, I.2) with a comment on how some famous contemporary poets, including himself, use speech in their poetry.

7. *Pavanadūta of Dhoyī*, edited by C. Chakravarti (Calcutta: Sanskrit Sahitya Parishad, 1926). This is modeled on the *Meghadūta* of Kālidāsa; here Kuvalayavatī, a nymph from the Malaya hills, sends the wind (*pavana*), instead of a cloud (*megha*), as a messenger to Lakṣmaṇasena.

8. See Pischel, "Die Hofdichter"; Monmohan Chakravarti, "Sanskrit Literature during the Sena Rule," *Journal of the Asiatic Society of Bengal*, n.s., 2, no. 5 (1906),

157–76; S. C. Mukherji, *Vaiṣṇavism in Bengal*, pp. 71–83; D. K. Mukherji, "Identification of some Verses by Umāpatidhara found in Two Inscriptions of Lakṣmaṇasena," *Journal of the Asiatic Society of Bengal*, 4th ser., 9, nos. 3–4 (1967), 188–92. Some verses from the *Āryāsaptaśatī* of Govardhana are translated in section five of this study; texts are given in note 35 to that section. The following verse is quoted in the Durgāprasad and Parab edition of the text, Kāvyamālā, no. 1 (Bombay: Nirṇayasāgara Press, 1886), p. 1:

> *govardhanaś ca śaraṇo jayadeva umāpatiḥ |*
> *kavirājaś ca ratnāni samitau lakṣmaṇasya ca ||*

This is reported to have been seen by Caitanya's disciple Sanātana Gosvāmin in an inscription over the assembly hall at Lakṣmaṇasena's capital of Navadvipa. It is otherwise unnoticed.

9. Royal patronage of Sanskrit language and literature at the court of Lakṣmaṇasena was linked to a renaissance of Sanskrit in northern India during the tenth, eleventh, and twelfth centuries. The courts of Bengal, Orissa, Kashmir, Kanauj, and Dhāra were notable among centers of brahmanical scholarship and literary activity. Scholars and poets traveled extensively in the quest for patronage. Their philosophical, religious, and literary products were as complex and highly eclectic as the great Hindu temples that marked the style of the period. See K. K. Handiqui, *Yaśastilaka and Indian Culture* (Sholapur: Jaina Saṁskṛti Saṁrakshaka Sangha, 1949); R. C. Majumdar, et al., *The Age of Imperial Kanauj* and *The Struggle for Empire*, vols. IV and V in *The History and Culture of the Indian People* (Bombay: Bharatiya Vidya Bhavan, 1955, 1957). Inscriptions of Vākpati-Muñja, the Paramāra ruler of Malwa at the end of the tenth century, make reference to the presence of brahmans who have migrated all the way from Bengal; see section five of this study, note 28. We also know from the poet's biographical sketch in his *Vikramāṅkadevacarita* that Bilhaṇa traveled from Kashmir in the latter part of the eleventh century to serve as the court poet of Vikramāditya VI, the Chalukya king of Kalyani (in modern Karnataka); see Barbara Stoler Miller, *Phantasies of a Love-Thief: The Caurapañcāśikā Attributed to Bilhaṇa* (New York: Columbia University Press, 1971), pp. 188–91; Helen Waddell, *The Wandering Scholars* (New York: Barnes and Noble, 1949).

10. N. G. Majumdar, ed., *Inscriptions of Bengal* (Rajshahi, Bengal: Varendra Research Society, 1929), vol. 3, pp. 81–172; for reference to other inscriptions, see R. C. Majumdar, *History of Ancient Bengal*, p. 231 and notes. It is notable that *auṁ namo nārāyaṇāya* is the principal mantra of the Śrīvaishnava cult. See Otto Schrader, *Introduction to the Pāñcarātra and the Ahirbudhnya Saṁhitā* (Madras: Adyar Library, 1916), pp. 141–43; see also S. N. Dasgupta, *A History of Indian Philosophy* (Cambridge: Cambridge University Press, 1961), vol. 3, pp. 12–21.

11. For a review of the accounts of Rāmānuja's life, see Dasgupta, *History of Indian Philosophy*, vol. 3, pp. 100–5. Dasgupta notes (p. 100n2): "Most of the details of Rāmānuja's life are collected from the account given in the *Prapannāmṛta* by Anantācārya, a junior contemporary of Rāmānuja."

12. J. F. Fleet, "Sanskrit and Old-Kanarese Inscriptions: Grants of Anantavarma-Choḍagaṅgadeva," *The Indian Antiquary*, 18 (1889), 161–76. The most detailed analysis of the reign of Choḍagaṅgadeva is in H. K. Mahtab, *History of Orissa* (Cuttack: Prajatantra Prachar Samity, 1959), pp. 196–211; a list of inscriptions by and referring to Choḍagaṅgadeva is given on pp. 209–211. See also Prabhat Mukherji, *The History of Medieval Vaishnavism in Orissa* (Calcutta: R. Chatterji,

1 *Jayadeva: The Wandering Poet (cont.)*

1940); S. N. Rajaguru, *History of the Gaṅgas* (Bhubaneswar: State Museum, 1968), K. C. Miśra, *The Cult of Jagannātha* (Calcutta: K. L. Mukhopadhyay, 1971), pp. 40–42. In a late thirteenth century copper-plate inscription of the Gaṅga king Narasiṁhadeva II, the construction of the Jagannātha temple and a Lakṣmī temple is attributed to Choḍagaṅgadeva; N. N. Vasu, "Copper-plate inscription of Nṛsiṁhadeva II of Orissa, dated 1217 Śaka," *Journal of the Asiatic Society of Bengal,* 65, pt. 1 (1896), 240 (text), 261 (trans.), vv. 27–28.

13. See Miśra, *Cult of Jagannātha.*

14. Monmohan Chakravarti, "Uriya Inscriptions of the 15th and 16th Centuries," *Journal of the Asiatic Society of Bengal,* 62, pt. 1 (1894), 88–104; see Miśra, *Cult of Jagannātha,* pp. 54–55.

15. Relevant portions of the *Caitanyacaritāmṛta* are quoted by S. K. De in *The Early History of the Vaiṣṇava Faith and Movement in Bengal* (Calcutta: K. L. Mukhopadhyay, 1961), p. 112; see also E. C. Dimock, Jr., *The Place of the Hidden Moon: Erotic Mysticism in the Vaiṣṇava-sahajīyā Cult of Bengal* (Chicago: University of Chicago Press, 1966), p. 55.

16. The *Bālabodhinī* commentary of Caitanyadāsa, a Bengali Vaishnava scholar and devotee who lived in Vṛndāvana in the late sixteenth century, gives this interpretation to the text; it is followed by Harekrishna Mukhopādhyāya in his introduction to his edition of the text and commentary, as well as by most contemporary Vaishnava writers on the *Gītagovinda.*

17. See Dimock, *Place of the Hidden Moon,* pp. 56–57; Shashibhushan Dasgupta, *Obscure Religious Cults* (Calcutta: K. L. Mukhopadhyay, 1969), pp. 115, 118.

18. See Miśra, *Cult of Jagannātha,* p. 149. Kali Charan Patnaik, the Oriya poet who has composed an Oriya lyric version of the *Gītagovinda* (Cuttack: Das, 1970) and from whom I have learned much about Oriya traditions surrounding the poem and its performance, holds the title "Gītagovinda-sevaka" in the Jagannātha temple of Puri. This means that he is responsible for the singing of the *daśavatāra* song before the image at every evening worship and various other songs at night.

19. Cited from R. K. Majumdar, "A 15th Century Gītagovinda Ms. with Gujaratī Paintings," *Journal of the University of Bombay, Arts and Law,* 6, no. 11, pt. 6 (1937), 127, with plate. The significance of this inscription is discussed below in relation to the critical text of the *Gītagovinda.*

20. These manuscripts form the basis of my critical edition of the *Gītagovinda;* they are described and analyzed in detail in the critical apparatus in the clothbound edition of this book. Evidence of the poem's status by the fourteenth century is the citation of verse III.11 as an example of the poetic figure *niścaya,* "certainty," in the tenth *pariccheda* of the *Sāhityadarpaṇa* of Viśvanātha, edited with notes by P. V. Kane (Delhi: Motilal Banarsidass, 1965), X.39.

21. See Kulkarni's edition of the text and commentary and my analysis of the early dated manuscripts of the Shorter Recension of the *Gītagovinda;* see also Majumdar, "15th Century Gītagovinda Ms."

22. See Telang and Panshikar edition; also R. C. Majumdar, et al., *The Delhi Sultanate,* vol. V in *The History and Culture of the Indian People* (Bombay: Bharatiya Vidya Bhavan, 1960), pp. 332–38; the introduction to Premlata Sharma's edition of

Saṅgītarāja by *Mahārāṇā Kumbhā* (Varanasi: Hindu University Press, 1963), vol. 1, pp. 29–70.

2 *The Lyrical Structure of Jayadeva's Poem*

1. I. A. Richards, *Practical Criticism* (New York: Harcourt, Brace, Harvest paperback, 1958), p. 200.

2. Because Jayadeva's songs are characterized by long compounds in which the relations among words are fluid, any translation of the *Gītagovinda* is necessarily tentative.

3. See Daniel H. H. Ingalls, *An Anthology of Sanskrit Court Poetry,* Harvard Oriental Series, vol. 44 (Cambridge, Mass.: Harvard University Press, 1965); Barbara Stoler Miller, *Bhartrihari: Poems* (New York: Columbia University Press, 1967).

4. See A. B. Keith, *A History of Sanskrit Literature* (Oxford: Oxford University Press, 1920), pp. 191–92; S. N. Dasgupta, ed., *A History of Sanskrit Literature, Classical Period* (Calcutta: University of Calcutta, 1947), pp. 392–95, 509–10; E. Gerow and A. K. Ramanujan, "Indian Poetics" and "The Lyric Poem" in *The Literatures of India,* edited by E. C. Dimock, Jr., et al. (Chicago: University of Chicago Press, 1974), pp. 138–41, 155–56. V. Raghavan, in his study *Bhoja's Śṛṅgāra Prakāśa* (Madras: Punarvasu, 1963), pp. 549–51, suggests that the *Gītagovinda* is a kind of musical poem that Bhoja calls *citrarāgakāvya,* a poem meant to be sung in several melodic patterns (*rāga*) and to be interpreted in the language of gesture (*abhinaya*). The classification of poems that are to be sung as *rāgakāvya* is known from Abhinavagupta's *Abhinavabhāratī* on the *Nāṭyaśāstra,* edited by M. R. Kavi, Gaekwad's Oriental Series, 4 vols. (Baroda: Central Library, 1956), vol. 1, pp. 174–84. Both Abhinavagupta and Bhoja recognize a variety of "nonclassical" forms and attempt to codify them within the classical categories. Their recognition suggests the existence of a poetic genre similar to the form of the *Gītagovinda* by the tenth century, but no works survive for comparison. See A. K. Warder, *Indian Kāvya Literature* (Delhi: Motilal Banarsidass, 1972), vol. 1, pp. 163–65.

5. These sound patterns occur in earlier Sanskrit works, but only sporadically. See Keith, *Sanskrit Literature,* pp. 197–98; Edwin Gerow, *A Glossary of Indian Figures of Speech* (The Hague: Mouton, 1971), pp. 102–7; Warder, *Kāvya Literature,* vol. 2, pp. 174–76.

6. "Song cycle" is an attempt to put the terms *prabandha* and *padāvalī,* as Jayadeva uses them, in a meaningful relation.

7. For examples of alliteration in the verses, see I.1, 35, 36; III.15, 20; V.19. The *Rasikapriyā* commentary offers the most complete analyses of the standard figures employed in individual verses; see Gerow, *Glossary.*

8. I use the terms *akṣaravṛtta* and *tālavṛtta,* following the nomenclature most commonly found in commentaries on the *Gītagovinda,* but the term *chandas* is sometimes found in place of *vṛtta* as the general word for meter. Thus syllabic meters are designated *akṣaravṛtta* as well as *akṣarachandas; varṇavṛtta* is also used. Moric meters are designated *mātravṛtta* and *mātrachandas,* as well as *tālavṛtta; gaṇachandas* is used of moric meters where the beats are organized into measured units (*gaṇa*). The metrical analysis presented here draws on the following studies: C. Lassen, *Gītagovinda* (Bonn, 1836), pp. xxvii–xxxv; Sudhibhushan Bhattacarya in Harekrishna Mukhopādhyāya's *Kavijayadeva o śrīgītagovinda* (Calcutta: Gurudās Mukhopādhyāy,

2 The Lyrical Structure of Jayadeva's Poem (cont.)

1957, B.S. 1363, pp. 230–41; Edwin Gerow's unpublished paper on Jayadeva's meters, delivered at the annual meeting of the American Oriental Society in 1966, which the author generously made available to me. Detailed discussions of Sanskrit, Prākrit, and Apabhraṁśa moric meters include: H. Jacobi, "Ueber die Entwicklung d. indischen Metrik in nachvedischer Zeit," *Zeitschrift der Deutsche Morgenländische Gesellschaft*, 38, (1884), 590–617; H. D. Velanker, "Apabhraṁśa Meters," *Journal of the University of Bombay, Arts and Law*, 2, pt. 3 (1933), 32–62 and 5, pt. 3 (1936) 41–93; "Prākṛta and Apabhraṁśa Meters," *Journal of the Bombay Branch of the Royal Asiatic Society*, 22 (1947), 15–32, and 23 (1947), 1–11; Sivaprasad Bhattacaryya, *Jottings on Sanskrit Metrics* (Calcutta: Sanskrit College, 1963), pp. 15 ff.

9. With the exception of the meter Śloka, which allows of considerable variation, and Puṣpitāgrā, which is a syllabic meter with paired quarters of unequal length (*ardhasamacatuṣpadī*), the syllabic meters in the *Gītagovinda* have quarter-stanzas of identical length and form (*samacatuṣpadī*). The meters are noted here in order of their frequency within the text:

Śardūlavikrīḍita (_ _ _ ⌣ ⌣ _ ⌣ _ ⌣ ⌣ ⌣ _ , _ _ ⌣ _ _ ⌣ _) I.1, 3, 16, 36, 46, 47; II.19; III.12, 13, 14; IV.10, 19, 21; V.7, 17, 18; VI.11; VII.11, 30; IX.10; X.13; XI.10, 11, 22; XII.10, 21.

Hariṇī (⌣ ⌣ ⌣ ⌣ ⌣ _ , _ _ _ _ , ⌣ _ ⌣ _ ⌣ _) II.1, 10; III.11; V.16, 19; VII.40; X.10, 12; XII.1, 20.

Vasantatilakā (_ _ ⌣ _ ⌣ ⌣ ⌣ _ ⌣ ⌣ _ ⌣ _ _) I.2, 25; III.15; VII.1, 41; X.1, 11; XI. 12, 13.

Śikhariṇī (⌣ _ _ _ _ _ , ⌣ ⌣ ⌣ ⌣ ⌣ _ _ ⌣ ⌣ ⌣ _) I.26; II.20; VIII.10; XI.32, 33.

Śloka (a and c, X X X X ⌣ _ _ ⌣ [either heavy or light], b and d, X X X X ⌣ _ ⌣ ⌣) III.1; IV.1; XI.23, XII.11.

Mālinī (⌣ ⌣ ⌣ ⌣ ⌣ ⌣ _ _ , _ ⌣ _ _ ⌣ _ _) I.35; VI.10; XI.1.

Puṣpitāgrā (a and c, ⌣ ⌣ ⌣ ⌣ ⌣ ⌣ _ ⌣ _ ⌣ _ _ , b and d, ⌣ ⌣ ⌣ ⌣ _ ⌣ ⌣ _ ⌣ _ ⌣ _ _) IV.22; V.1; VIII.1.

Vaṁśastha (⌣ _ ⌣ _ _ ⌣ ⌣ _ ⌣ _ ⌣ _) 1.37; III.2; VII.39.

Drutavilambita (⌣ ⌣ ⌣ _ ⌣ ⌣ _ ⌣ ⌣ _ ⌣ _) I.4; VII.21.

Upendravajrā (⌣ _ ⌣ _ _ ⌣ ⌣ _ ⌣ _ _) IV.20; VII.12.

Pṛthvī (⌣ _ ⌣ ⌣ ⌣ _ ⌣ _ , ⌣ ⌣ ⌣ _ ⌣ _ _ ⌣ _) X.14.

Upajāti (⌣ _ ⌣ _ _ ⌣ ⌣ _ ⌣ _ ⌣) XII.22.

Five of the meters are named by punning in verses where they occur: Śikhariṇī (II.20); Śārdūlavikrīḍita (IV.10), Puṣpitāgrā (IV.22), Upendravajrā (IV.20), Pṛthvī (X.14). This punning is further evidence of Jayadeva's interest in the integration of sense and sound.

10. See examples from the *Sattasaī* of Hāla quoted in note 21 to section 5; see also G. L. Hart, III, *The Poems of Ancient Tamil* (Berkeley: University of California Press, 1975), appendix I, "An Analysis of the Meter and Rhyme of the First Twenty-five Poems of the *Sattasaī*," pp. 281–84.

11. Āryā is expressed in couplets of seven and one-half measures. Most measures (*gaṇa*) consists of four beats, with the standard exception of the sixth measure of the second line, which has a single beat, making the two lines asymmetrical. Further restrictions in the syllabic patterns of certain other measures give Āryā a fairly

fixed form. The opening verse of the sixth *sarga* (VI.1) is an example of how Sanskrit syllables may be ordered in terms of this form:

atha tāṁ gantum aśaktāṁ ciram anuraktāṁ latāgrhe dr̥ṣṭvā |
taccaritaṁ govinde manasijamande sakhī prāha ||

‿‿− |−‿‿| −−|‿‿‿‿| −−|‿−‿| −−|−|
−‿‿ |−−|−−|‿‿‿‿‿| −−|‿| −−|‿||

Four-beat measures in the forms ‿‿‿‿, − −, −‿‿, or ‿‿− occur freely. The syllabic sequence ‿−‿ is restricted to the second and fourth measures of both lines, and to the sixth measure of the first line, in which the sequence ‿‿‿‿ is its only alternative. The eighth measure of each line is conventionally a heavy or light monosyllable. The frequency and position of heavy syllables, including the spondaic sequence (− −), is notable in comparison with the meters of the songs; the amphibrach sequence (‿ − ‿) occurs only a few times in refrain verses of the songs.

12. In the terminology of classical Indian music theory (*saṅgītaśāstra*), the songs are called *prabandha* (the term Jayadeva uses at I.2) or *gītabandha*. See V. G. Apte, ed., *Sāṅgītaratnākara,* Ānandāśrama Sanskrit Series, no. 35 (Poona: Ānandāśrama Press, 1942), chapter 4 (*prabandhādhyāya*), pp. 271–354. *Chandaḥprabandha* designates songs that are bound up in meter (*yati*), which provides their rhythmical component.

13. See note 3 to section 1 above—Pischel, p. 22; Chatterji, pp. 31–33. See also Louis Renou, et al., *L'Inde Classique* (Paris: Payot, 1949), vol. I, p. 443.

There is much confusion surrounding the use of the term "Apabhraṁśa." It is often broadly used to designate both forms and stages of Indo-Aryan language that differ from Sanskrit and the literary Prākrits. More specifically, it refers to a vernacular of western India that achieved literary form in the period ca. A.D. 600–1400. It was used by Jain writers in Gujarat and Rajasthan for the composition of poetry. A similar Prākrit, with its reduced inflections and increased postpositions, was used by Buddhist writers in Bengal and Orissa. See Richard Pischel, "Materialien zur Kenntnis des Apabhraṁśa," *Abhandlungen der. K. Gesellschaft der Wissenschaften zu Göttigen,* n.s., 5, no. 4 (1902); Ludwig Alsdorf, "Apabhraṁśa Studien," *Deutsche Morgenländische Gesellschaft,* 22, no. 2 (1937); Sukumar Sen, "Charyageetikosh," *Indian Linguistics,* 9 (1944–48), 30–133; G. V. Tagare, *Historical Grammar of Apabhraṁśa* (Poona: Deccan College, 1948); S. K. Chatterji, *The Origin and Development of the Bengali Language* (1926; reprint, London: Allen and Unwin, 1970), vol. I, pp. 109–29; S. M. Katre, *Prakrit Languages and their Contribution to Indian Culture* (Poona: Deccan College, 1964), pp. 21, 24, 84–89; Shashibhusan Dasgupta, "The Buddhist Sahajiyā Cult," in *Obscure Religious Cults* (Calcutta: K. L. Mukhopadhyay, 1969), pp. 3–9 ff. It is worth noting that Jayadeva's rhyming moric meters, like the rhyming moric meters of the Caryā songs, are reflected in the meters of later Bengali and Oriya poetry, e.g., Payāra and Tripadī: see Sen, "Charyageetikosh," p. 125. The couplets of the *Gītagovinda* songs should also be compared with verses found in C. M. Ghose, ed., *Prākrtapaiṅgala.* (Calcutta: Asiatic Society of Bengal, 1902), a treatise on Prākrit and Apabhraṁśa versification. Examples are drawn from the floating mass of popular poetry of North India during the period ca. A.D. 900–1400; see vv. 334, 570, 576, 581, 586.

14. For example, the tenth-century Jain author Somadeva applied Prākrit and Apabhraṁśa meters to Sanskrit in his *Yaśastilakacampū* (edited by Śivadatta and

2 The Lyrical Structure of Jayadeva's Poem (cont.)

Parab, Kāvyamālā, no. 70; Bombay: Nirṇayasāgara Press, 1903). In the "Kṛṣṇāvatāra" chapter of Kṣemendra's Daśāvatāracarita (VIII.173, quoted below in note 30 to section 5), the narrative is interrupted by a song sung by the cowherdesses in four lines of long, end-rhymed compounds, set in a rhythm of ten four-beat measures followed by a heavy syllable, and so resembles the metrical structure of the Gītagovinda songs. It is notable that both of these works are among the scattered sources antedating Jayadeva that contain references to Rādhā (see section 5). If one accepts the convincing argument of H. D. Velankar in favor of the authenticity of the Apabhraṁśa stanzas in the fourth act of the Vikramorvaśīya of Kālidāsa, there is an even earlier example of Apabhraṁśa stanzas, and stanzas in a more conventional Prākrit, used in conjunction with Sanskrit forms; see H. D. Velankar, ed., The Vikramorvaśīya of Kālidāsa (Delhi: Sahitya Akademi, 1961), pp. lvi–lxxx, 61–91. See also W. Caland, "Een onbekend Indisch tooneelstuk (Gopālakelicandrikā)," Verhandelingen der Koninklijke Akademie van Wetenschappen te Amsterdam, 17, no. 3 (1917), 1–158; cf. review by Sten Konow in the Indian Antiquary, 49 (1920), 232–36; M. Winternitz, "Kṛṣṇa-dramen," Zeitschrift der Deutschen Morgenländischen Gesellschaft, 74 (1920), 137–44.

15: This meter is identified by the commentator Kumbhakarṇa as Layachandas; see Kumbha's Saṅgītarāja, edited by P. Sharma (Varanasi: Hindu University Press, 1963), I.3.21; see also, H. D. Velankar, "Hemacandra's Chandonuśāsana," Journal of the Bombay Branch of the Royal Asiatic Society, 20 (1944), 29 (VII.4). The same meter occurs in songs 4, 5, 6, 8, 11, 17, 20, 22, and 23. Several other meters patterned in four-beat measures are only variants of Layachandas. The meter of the first song has couplets in unequal lines of sixteen and twenty beats; it is identified by Kumbha as Kīrtidhavalachandas and is defined in the Saṅgītarāja (I.3.36). The meter of songs 9, 12, 14, and 18 has couplets of four four-beat measures. The meter of song 16 has three four-beat measures followed by a trochaic cadence ($_ \smile$). The meter of song 15 has six four-beat measures followed by an iambic cadence ($\smile _$). The meter of song 24 has six four-beat measures followed by a cretic cadence ($_ \smile _$). The less regular meter of the second song, which Kumbha calls Maṅgalachandas and defines in the Saṅgītarāja (I.3.39), has couplets in unequal lines of twenty and eleven beats, the first line consisting of five four-beat measures and the second line of two four-beat measures followed by a trochaic cadence ($_ \smile$).

16. The four-beat measures are expressed predominantly in two out of five possible syllabic combinations of groups of four beats: four light syllables ($\smile \smile \smile \smile$) or a heavy syllable followed by two light syllables ($_ \smile \smile$). Given the syllabic structure of Sanskrit, with the prominence of consonant clusters and heavy vowels, the control that Jayadeva exercises on the placement of heavy syllables is masterful. A measure of two heavy syllables ($_ _$) normally occurs only in final position in a line of a couplet; a measure of two light syllables followed by a heavy syllable ($\smile \smile _$) is rare; and no measure with a heavy syllable between two light syllables ($\smile _ \smile$) occurs.

Of the remaining five songs in the Gītagovinda, three have meters based on measures of five beats, one has a meter that is best resolved into measures of seven beats, and another is entirely irregular. The five-beat meters generally show the same preference for light syllables and the same restriction of heavy syllables to initial position within a measure that characterize the four-beat meters. The combinations of five light syllables ($\smile \smile \smile \smile \smile$) or a heavy syllable followed by three light syllables (‿ ◡ ◡ ◡) are predominant. The meter of song 13 has couplets of four five-beat measures, the last of which is a cretic cadence (‿ ◡ ‿). The meter of song 19 has couplets of six five-beat measures followed by a spondaic cadence (‿ ‿); the cretic pattern (‿ ◡ ‿) in the fourth measure of almost every line gives this long meter a distinctive rhythm. The meter of song 21 has couplets of three five-beat measures, but the first line of each couple is lengthened by the addition of a final heavy syllable. The meter of song 7 divides into three seven-beat measures in the fixed sequence ‿ ◡ ‿ ◡ ◡ , followed by a trochaic cadence (‿ ◡). Song 10 is expressed in five metrically identical verses of asymmetrical quarter-stanzas. The quarter-stanzas all differ in syllable sequence and moric length, while consistently rhyming in the pattern *a b/a b*. The first verse of the song shows the fixed pattern:

> *vahati malayasamīre madanam upanidhāya* |
> *sphuṭati kusumanikare virahahṛdayadalanāya* ||
>
> ◡ ◡ ◡ ◡ ◡ ◡ ◡ – – , ◡ ◡ ◡ ◡ ◡ ◡ – ◡ |
> ◡ ◡ ◡ ◡ ◡ ◡ ◡ – , ◡ ◡ ◡ ◡ ◡ ◡ – ◡ ||

17. The Nepal manuscript dated A.D. 1447 and the Bombay manuscript dated A.D. 1515 omit *tāla* names. The frequent designation *yatitāla* in other manuscripts may perhaps be interpreted as "the *tāla* of the meter," meaning that the meter is the *tāla*. On *tāla*, see Alain Daniélou, *Northern Indian Music* (New York: Praeger, 1968), pp. 65–74; P. Sambamoorthy, *South Indian Music,* book II (Madras: Indian Music Publishing House, 1968), pp. 18–28; Ravi Shankar, *My Music, My Life* (New York: Simon and Schuster, 1968), pp. 29–30.

18. The refrains whose measured unit differs from the *gaṇa* organization of the couplets in the song may be resolved as follows:
SONG 9: two measures of seven beats, followed by a light syllable; cf. song 7, which
  also seems to follow a *saptagaṇa* pattern, a rarity in Indian prosody.
SONG 10: four measures of four beats, followed by two light syllables.
SONG 14: four measures of five beats, followed by a heavy syllable.
SONG 15: four measures of six beats, followed by a heavy syllable.
SONG 18: begins with a trochaic unit of heavy-light (‿ ◡), followed by four measures of four beats, like the meter of the couplets.
SONG 22: one line has five measures of four beats, the second line begins with a unit of eight beats (‿ ◡ ‿ ◡ ◡ ◡), followed by five measures of four beats.

19. There are more heavy syllables in the four-beat measures of the refrains: the spondaic unit of two heavy syllables (‿ ‿) and the anapestic unit of two light syllables followed by a heavy syllable (◡ ◡ ‿) occur in the interior of lines, e.g. song 16 (VII.31, refrain). The amphibrach unit of a heavy syllable between two light syllables, which is nowhere used in the four-beat meters of the couplets, occurs in the refrains of songs 1, 4, 7, 17, 20, and 24.

20. See Gerow, *Glossary,* pp. 102–7. It should be noted that the repetition of consonant clusters is minimal in the *Gītagovinda,* suggesting comparison with Prākrit and Apabhraṁśa, where the clusters are normally reduced; see Gerow on *grāmyānuprāsa, Glossary,* p. 103.

21. For example, II.5:

> *vipulapu* | *lakabhuja* | *pallava* | *valayita* | *ballava* | *yuvatisa* | *hasram* |
> ◡ ◡ ◡ ◡ | ◡ ◡ ◡ ◡ | – ◡ ◡ | ◡ ◡ ◡ ◡ | – ◡ ◡ | ◡ ◡ ◡ ◡ | – – |
> *karacara* | *norasi* | *maṇigaṇa* | *bhūṣaṇa* | *kiraṇavi* | *bhinnata* | *masram* ||
> ◡ ◡ ◡ ◡ | – ◡ ◡ | ◡ ◡ ◡ ◡ | – ◡ ◡ | ◡ ◡ ◡ ◡ | – ◡ ◡ | – – ||

2 The Lyrical Structure of Jayadeva's Poem (cont.)

22. An early instance of the use of *antānuprāsa* is the sixth *sarga* of *Sundarakāṇḍa* in the *Vālmīkirāmāyaṇa*. Though the date of this section is debated by scholars, it is accepted in the critical edition; see G. C. Jhala, ed., *Vālmīkirāmāyaṇa* (Baroda: Oriental Institute, 1966), vol. 5, pp. 76–80.

23. See K. Krishnamoorthy, ed., *Dhvanyāloka* (Dharwar: Karnatak University, 1974), II.14–15.

24. See, e.g., Daṇḍin, *Kāvyadarśa*, edited by V. N. Ayer (Madras: Ramaswamy Sastrulu, 1964) I.51–60; Daṇḍin discusses *anuprāsa* in the context of delineating the differences between the two major styles of poetry, called *vaidarbhī-rīti* and *gauḍī-rīti* (I.40–54). The *gauḍī* style was located in eastern India; its exponents were noted for their love of *anuprāsa*. See also Bhoja, *Sarasvatīkaṇṭhābharaṇa* (Bombay: Nir-ṇayasāgara Press, 1934) II.76, 77, 106; Jagannātha, *Rasagaṅgadhāra* (Bombay: Nir-ṇayasāgara Press, 1939), p. 89.

25. See note 9 above.

26. See section 4 below. For other examples of Jayadeva's word-play, see *rasana, rasa, rasita* in song 14 (VII.16, 17); and *hari, hara, hāra* in song 20 (XI.6). Song 19, which begins the climax of the poem, has rich word-play on various levels. Puns in verse I.36, in the long compound *dhyānāvadhānakṣaṇaprāptaprāṇasamāsamāgamara-sollāsa* which modifies *pathika*, relate yogic meditation to lonely travelers' evocation of erotic union.

27. See Gerow, *Glossary*, on *anuprāsa* (pp. 102–7), *citra* (pp. 175–89), *yamaka* (pp. 223–38).

28. See Stella Kramrisch, *The Hindu Temple*, 2 vols. (Calcutta, 1946). The inter-play of "surface beauty" and underlying structure is also characteristic of Indian dance and music.

29. My initial appreciation of the music of the *Gītagovinda* came from many hours of listening to singers in various regions of India render their versions of the songs. A deeper appreciation is based on formal study under the tutelage of Vasant Rai, Director of the Alam school of Indian Music in New York, who belongs to the tradition of Allaudin Khan, and under V. Deshikachar at the Mysore College of Fine Arts. This attempt to define the *rāga* draws on Ravi Shankar's exposition in *My Music, My Life*. See also Daniélou, *Northern Indian Music*, pp. 20–63, 75–96ff.; N. A. Jairazbhoy, *The Rāgs of North Indian Music: Their Structure and Evolution* (London: Faber and Faber, 1971); Walter Kaufmann, *The Ragas of North India* (Bloomington: Indiana University Press, 1968); Sambamoorthy, *South Indian Music*, books I–V; V. G. Apte, ed., *Saṅgītaratnākara* (Poona: Ānandāśrama Press, 1942), 2 vols.

30. The northern versions of the songs, as I heard them in Orissa and Bengal, fol-low the *rāga* designations most commonly found in the manuscripts; these differ from those of Kumbhakarṇa, which are defined in his *Saṅgītarājā*. In articles writ-ten for the "Geet Govind Celebrations" held at the Sangeet Natak Akademi in Delhi (March 18–20, 1967), Premlata Sharma and C. S. Pant both suggest that the *rāgas* and *tālas* Kumbha prescribes were associated with his own compositions. The South Indian versions of the songs, as I heard them in Madras, Mysore, and Guru-vayor (Kerala), accord with the *rāgas* given by Semmangudi R. Sreenivasa Iyer in *Gītagovindam with Musical Notations* (Tripunithura: Sanskrit College, 1962). The

designations in the present text of the *Gītagovinda* are those common to the oldest manuscripts; significant variants are noted in the critical apparatus in the clothbound edition of this book. For a comparison of the musical characteristics associated with different *rāgas* of the Hindusthani and Karnatak systems, see B. Subba Rao, *Rāganidhi* (Madras: Music Academy, 1964–66), vols. I–IV.

3 *Jayadeva's Language for Love*

1. The background for this analysis is provided by the *rasa* theory of dramatic esthetics in its general form. The relation between esthetic experience and religious experience that is central to the *Gītagovinda* encouraged me to search for evidence of Jayadeva's direct reference to the special theories of Abhinavagupta or Bhoja, but the vocabulary of esthetics that Jayadeva uses is drawn directly from the *Nāṭyaśāstra*. The technical terminology of *dhvani* theory and *śṛṅgāra* theory is notably absent; individual terms are analyzed in the glossary to the hardcover edition. For a general introduction to basic notions of Indian literary esthetics, see Edward C. Dimock, Jr., et al., *The Literatures of India* (Chicago: The University of Chicago Press, 1974), chapter 3. Within Sanskrit literature, the *rasa* theory is summarized in book 4 of Dhanaṁjaya's *Daśarūpa*, translated, with Sanskrit text and notes, by G. C. O. Haas (reprint, Delhi: Motilal Banarsidass, 1962), pp. 106–48. The summary is based on book 7 of Bharata's *Nāṭyaśāstra*, edited, with the commentary of Abhinavagupta, by M. R. Kavi, Gaekwad's Oriental Series, 4 vols. (Baroda: Central Library, 1926), vol. I, pp. 343–86.

2. Bhoja, in his *Śṛṅgāraprakāśa*, concentrated on *rati* and the *śṛṅgāra* developing from it. He expanded and further universalized *śṛṅgāra* into an absolute *rasa* called *ahaṁkāraśṛṅgāra*, a rarefication of ordinary love which is for him the universal of existence; see V. Raghavan, *Bhoja's Śṛṅgāra Prakāśa* (Madras: Punarvasu, 1963), pp. 425–532. Earlier, Rudraṭa had expressed the more general view of the importance of *rati* and *śṛṅgāra* by raising the question of how any other *rasa* except *śṛṅgāra* could be truly relished and how the name *rasa* could apply to any sentiment but *śṛṅgāra; Kāvyālaṁkāra* XIV.38 says:

> *anusarati rasānaṁ rasyatāmasya nānyaḥ*
> *sakalam idam anena vyāptam ābālavṛddham.*

See S. K. De, *Ancient Indian Erotics and Erotic Literature* (Calcutta: K. L. Mukhopadhyay, 1959).

3. A conventionalized blending of the two modes is made in the *adyāpi smarāmi* formula that dominates the *Caurapañcāśikā* attributed to Bilhaṇa; see my *Phantasies of a Love-Thief* (New York: Columbia University Press, 1971). The interplay of the two modes is dominant in Indian literature from the epic period, as well as later. Outstanding examples include the *Nalopakhyāna* of the *Mahabhārata*, the *Vālmīkirāmāyaṇa*, and Kālidāsa's *Kumārasaṁbhava*, as well as his plays.

4. See the introduction to my translation *Bhartrihari: Poems* (New York: Columbia University Press, 1967). It seems significant to me that the esthetic presentation of emotion in the *Gītagovinda* can be characterized by the same generalizations that I applied to the Bhartṛhari collection.

5. The earliest known critic to contrast what is vulgar (*grāmya*) from what is conducive to *rasa* was Daṇḍin, in his *Kāvyadarśa*, edited and translated by V. N.

3 *Jayadeva's Language for Love* (cont.)

Ayer (Madras: Ramaswamy Sastrulu, 1964), I.62–64. Abhinavagupta used the example of the breasts of a woman exciting most profoundly when they are only half revealed; in the *Dhvanyālokalocana* (edited with the *Bālapriyā;* Varanasi: Kashi Sanskrit Series, 1940), p. 138, he says:

> . . . *gopyamānaṁ sannāyikākucayugalam*
> *iva mahārghatam upayad dhvanyate* ||

The material is taken from J. L. Masson, "Obscenity in Sanskrit Literature," *Mahfil*, 7, nos. 3–4 (1971), pp. 197–207.

6. See J. L. Masson and M. V. Patwardhan, *Śāntarasa and Abhinavagupta's Philosophy of Aesthetics* (Poona: Bhandarkar Oriental Research Institute, 1969), pp. 56 ff.

7. The perspective of the friend is later codified into the elaborate esthetic theory of *sakhībhāva* in Bengali Vaishnavism; for the relevance of this theory to the *Gītagovinda*, see Shashibhusan Dasgupta, *Obscure Religious Cults* (Calcutta: K. L. Mukhopadhyay, 1969), pp. 125–26.

8. The technical term for such an opening verse is *vastunirdeśa*. It is possible that the much-debated phrase *nanda-nideśatah* is Jayadeva's pun on the type of this verse, referring to the fact that the subject of the poem is *nanda*, "joy," which is experienced as Krishna himself in the final song of the *Gītagovinda*, where he is addressed by the two epithets *Yadunandana* and *Hṛdayānandana*.

9. In his *Kavijayadeva o śrīgītagovinda* (Calcutta: Gurudās Mukhopādhyāy, 1957, B.S. 1362), Harekrishna Mukhopādhyāya devotes an entire chapter (15) to the analysis of this verse. Each of the commentators gives it detailed consideration.

10. Kumbhakarṇa gives an elaborate statement on poetic propriety in support of this interpretation. He glosses *nandanideśatah* with *nandasamīpāt*. He points to the combination of *śṛṅgāra* and *bhayanaka* here.

11. Mānāṅka interprets the speech as the *svagatam* of Rādhā, spoken from excessive love, as an alternative to understanding Nanda as the speaker.

12. This is the most frequent interpretation. It is related to the story that the child Krishna followed Nanda into the woods one evening at dusk and became afraid. Śankaramiśra gives this story in its simplest form. See Suniti Kumar Chatterji, *Jayadeva, Makers of Indian Literature* (New Delhi: Sahitya Akademi, 1973), pp. 15–18.

13. Caitanyadāsa explains that the words spoken by Rādhā's friend are intended to bring joy (*nanda*); Krishna's foster father is thus removed from any involvement with the erotic relationship between Rādhā and Krishna and is replaced by the conventional figure of the *sakhī*.

14. Cf. *Bṛhadāraṇyaka Upaniṣad* I.4.2:

so' bibhet tasmād ekākī bibheti sa hāyam īkṣāṁ cakre yan mad anyan nāsti kaṣmān nu bibhemīti tata evāsya bhayaṁ vīyāya kaṣmād hy abheṣyat dvitīyād vai bhayaṁ bhavati.

He was afraid. Therefore one who is alone is afraid. This one then thought to himself, "since there is nothing else than myself, of what am I afraid?" Thereupon his fear, verily, passed away, for of what should he have been afraid? Assuredly it is from a second that fear arises.

Introduction 50

Text and translation quoted from S. Radhakrishnan, *The Principal Upaniṣads* (New York: Harper, 1953), pp. 163–64. Although there is no evidence that Jayadeva consciously refers to this analysis of fear in the creative process, the dynamic role of fear in connecting isolation with pairing seems suggestive in interpreting the opening verse of the *Gītagovinda*.

15. In the second half of the poem it is increasingly clear that Krishna himself is the mysterious power of darkness, the essence of night in which Rādhā's love develops through various stages of desertion to consummation.

16. Mānāṅka makes the point, which is followed by other commentators, that the word order of the dual compound is irregular in its priority (*pūrvanipāta*), like *naranārāyaṇau, umāmaheśvarau, kākamayūrau,* etc.

17. See section I above, notes 15–17. The subject of allegory, with reference to the *Gītagovinda*, is treated by Lee Siegel in "Sacred and Profane Dimensions of Love in Indian Traditions as Exemplified in the *Gītagovinda* of Jayadeva" (unpublished Ph.D. thesis, Oxford University, 1975), pp. 209–25; also in the short essay by Ranajit Sarkar, "*Gītagovinda*: Towards a Total Understanding," *Publikaties van het Instituut voor Indische talen en culturen,* no. 2, Rijksuniversiteit te Groningen, 1974.

4 Krishna: Cosmic Cowherd Lover

1. A selected bibliography of references relevant to interpreting Jayadeva's treatment of Krishna includes: R. G. Bhandarkar, *Collected Works,* vol. IV: *Vaiṣṇavism, Śaivism, and Minor Religious Systems,* edited by N. B. Utgikar (Poona: Bhandarkar Oriental Research Institute, 1929); Shashibhusan Dasgupta, *Obscure Religious Cults* (1946; 2d ed., Calcutta: K. L. Mukhopadhyay, 1962—references throughout are to this edition); S. K. De, *Vaiṣṇava Faith and Movement in Bengal* (Calcutta: K. L. Mukhopadhyay, 1961); Franklin Edgerton, *The Bhagavad Gītā,* part 2, Harvard Oriental Series, vol. 39 (Cambridge, Mass.: Harvard University Press, 1952); Jan Gonda, *Aspects of Early Viṣṇuism* (1954; reprint, Delhi: Motilal Banarsidass, 1969); idem., *Viṣṇuism and Śivaism: A Comparison* (London: Athlone Press, 1970); E. Washburn Hopkins, *Epic Mythology* (1915; reprint, New York: Biblo and Tannen, 1969); Daniel H. H. Ingalls, "The Harivaṁśa as a Mahākāvya," in *Mélanges d'Indianisme à la mémoire de L. Renou* (Paris: Boccard, 1968), pp. 381–94; Hermann Jacobi, "Incarnation," *Encyclopedia of Religion and Ethics,* edited by James Hastings (Edinburgh, 1908–26), vol. VII, pp. 193–97; D. D. Kosambi, "The Avatāra Syncretism and Possible Sources of the Bhagavad-gītā," *Journal of the Bombay Branch of the Royal Asiatic Society,* n.s., 24 (1949), 121–34; idem., *Myth and Reality* (Bombay: Popular Prakashan, 1962), pp. 12–41; B. Majumdar, *Kṛṣṇa in History and Legend* (Calcutta: University of Calcutta, 1969); J. L. Masson, "The Childhood of Kṛṣṇa," *Journal of the American Oriental Society,* 94 (1974), 454–59; K. C. Miśra, *The Cult of Jagannātha* (Calcutta: K. L. Mukhopdhyay, 1971); Walter Ruben, *Krishna: Konkordanz und Kommentar der Motives seines Heldenlebens*(Istanbul, 1944); Milton Singer, ed., *Krishna: Myths, Rites, and Attitudes* (Honolulu: East-West Center, 1966); S. N. Tadpatrikar, "The Kṛṣṇa Problem," *Annals of the Bhandarkar Oriental Research Institute,* 10, (1931), 296–344; Charlotte Vaudeville, "Aspects du mythe de Kṛṣṇa-Gopāla dans l'Inde ancienne," in *Mélanges L. Renou,* pp. 737–61.

Most of the major Indian mythological themes are woven into Krishna's total legend, with the exception of asceticism. The absence of asceticism in Krishna's

4 *Krishna: Cosmic Cowherd Lover* (*cont.*)

legend is focal to the contrast between him and Śiva; see Wendy O'Flaherty, *Asceticism and Eroticism in the Mythology of Śiva* (London: Oxford University Press, 1973).

2. The main sources for Krishna's legend in early Sanskrit literature are the *Mahābhārata* and certain Purāṇas, but the origins of many of his epithets and characteristics are found in Vedic literature. The following texts are referred to throughout this section in the editions cited:

Atharva Veda. Atharvaveda Saṁhitā, edited by W. D. Whitney and R. Roth (Berlin: F. Dummler, 1856); translated by W. D. Whitney (1905; reprint, Delhi: Motilal Banarsidass, 1962).

Bhāgavata Purāṇa. Gita Press edition (Gorakhpur, 1962); translated into French by Eugène Burnouf, 5 vols. (Paris: Imprimerie Royale, 1840–98) and into English by J. M. Sanyal, 5 vols. (Calcutta: Oriental Publishing and Datta Bose, 1930–34).

Harivaṁśa. Critical edition, edited by P. L. Vaidya, 2 vols. (Poona: Bhandarkar Oriental Research Institute, 1969); translated into French by S. A. Langlois (London: Parbury, Allen, 1834–35).

Mahābhārata. Critical edition, edited by V. S. Sukthankar, et al. (Poona: Bhandarkar Oriental Research Institute, 1933–66); translated by J.A.B. van Buitenen (Chicago: University of Chicago Press, 1973–   ), vols. 1 and 2, books 1–3.

Matsya Purāṇa. Edited by H. N. Apte, Ānandāśrama Sanskrit Series, no. 54 (Poona: Ānandāśrama Press, 1907); translated in the Sacred Books of the Hindus, vol. 17 (Allahabad: Pāṇini Office, 1916–17; reprint, New York, 1973).

Ṛg Veda. The Hymns of the Rig-Veda, edited by Max Müller, 2 vols. (London: Trübner, 1877); translated into German by K. F. Geldner, 3 vols., Harvard Oriental Series, vols. 33–35 (Cambridge, Mass.: Harvard University Press, 1951).

Śatapatha Brāhmaṇa. Edited by Albrecht Weber (1855; reprint, Varanasi: Chowkhamba Sanskrit Series Office, 1964); translated by Julius Eggeling, Sacred Books of the East, vols. 12, 26, 41, 43, 44 (1882; reprint, Delhi: Motilal Banarsidass, 1964).

Viṣṇu Purāṇa. Gita Press edition (Gorakhpur, 1962); translated by H. H. Wilson, 5 vols. (1840; reprint, Calcutta, 1961).

3. *Mahābhārata* VI.33.30 = *Bhagavadgītā* 11.30.

4. See Gonda, *Aspects of Viṣṇuism,* p. 159; Hopkins, *Epic Mythology,* p. 213.

5. See *Viṣṇu P.* VI.2.17, where it says that singing of Keśava is the way of the Kali Yuga.

6. See J. Gonda, *Epithets in the Ṛgveda* (The Hague: Mouton, 1959).

7. The contrast between the conception of Krishna in the *Gītagovinda* and in the *Bhāgavata P.* is striking in terms of vocabulary and devotional attitude; see Thomas J. Hopkins, "The Social Teaching of the *Bhāgavata Purāṇa"* and J.A.B. van Buitenen, "On the Archaism of the *Bhāgavata Purāṇa,"* both in Singer, *Krishna,* pp. 3–40; also Tadpatrikar, "Kṛṣṇa Problem."

8. See section 5 below.

9. Daniel H. H. Ingalls, *An Anthology of Sanskrit Court Poetry,* Harvard Oriental Series, vol. 44 (Cambridge, Mass.: Harvard University Press, 1965), intr. 6.2, p. 93.

10. *Śatapatha Brāhmaṇa* XI.5.4.18; cf. the "honey-doctrine" of the *Bṛhadāraṇyaka Upaniṣad* II.5.16–19. In classical Hindu law a celibate student (*brahmacārin*) is ordered to abstain from "honey, meat, perfumes, garlands, condiments, women, etc.," *Manusmṛti* II.177; see *The Laws of Manu*, translated by G. Bühler, Sacred Books of the East, vol. 25 (Oxford: Clarendon Press, 1886), p. 62.

11. See Claude Lévi-Strauss, *From Honey to Ashes, Introduction to a Science of Mythology,* (New York: Harper and Row, 1973), vol. 2, pp. 122–23. In Indian literature, spring itself is considered an aphrodisiac; see, e.g., Kālidāsa's *Kumārasaṁbhava,* critical edition, edited by Suryakanta (New Delhi: Sahitya Akademi, 1962), III.21–34.

12. *Mādhava* and *Madhusūdana* are both commonly used of Krishna throughout the *Mahābhārata* and after; e.g., *Mahābhārata* I.213.20, 30 ff., 214.15 ff.; cf. Gonda, *Aspects of Viṣṇuism,* pp. 16 ff., 237; Hopkins, *Epic Mythology,* pp. 192–93, 203; G. Dumézil, *The Destiny of a King* (Chicago: The University of Chicago Press, 1973), pp. 81–83. A legend given in the *Nāṭyaśāstra,* edited and translated by M. Ghosh (Calcutta: Granthalaya, 1967), XXII.1–16, attributes the origin of drama to Krishna's battle with the demons Madhu and Kaitabha.

13. See, e.g., *Harivaṁśa* 48.1 ff.;. *Mahābhārata* I.1.60.

14. See, e.g., *Ṛg Veda* X.96; Gonda, *Aspects of Viṣṇuism,* p. 107.

15. Cf. *Mahābhārata* I.1.20–22, VI.33.9 (= *Bhagavadgītā* 11.9), VI.40.77 (= *BG* 18.77).

16. See, e.g., *Bhāgavata P.* X.37.

17. See Krishna as *Jagannivāsa, Mahābhārata* VI.33.25, 37 (= *BG* XI.25, 37); see Miśra, *Cult of Jagannātha,* pp. 57–58; section 1, note 14 above.

18. See *Mahābhārata* VI.26.5–9 (= *BG* IV.5–9); *Matsya P.* 47.8 ff.; *Viṣṇu P.* V.17.10 ff.; *Bhāgavata P.* II.6.41. Earlier references to the ten incarnations include: *Matsya P.* 285.6–7 (*matsyaḥ ḳurmo varāhaś ca narasiṁho 'tha vāmanaḥ rāmo rāmaś ca ḳṛṣṇaś ca buddhaḥ ḳalḳīti ca ḳramāt*); Kṣemendra, *Daśāvatāracarita,* Kāvyamālā, no. 26 (Bombay: Nirṇayasāgara Press, 1891); see also H. K. Sastri, "Two Statues of Pallava Kings and Five Pallava Inscriptions in a Rock-Temple at Mahabalipuram," *Memoirs of the Archaeological Survey of India,* no. 26, plate I, C, p. 5; "An Ajmer Stone Inscription," *Epigraphica Indica,* vol. 29, pp. 179 ff. The *Harivaṁśa* list (ch. 31) differs somewhat. In the list of twenty-two incarnations in the *Bhāgavata P.,* the pair Balarāma and Krishna are nineteenth and twentieth (I.3.23; cf. II.7). See Gonda, *Aspects of Viṣṇuism,* pp. 124–64; Hopkins, *Epic Mythology,* pp. 209–19; Jacobi, "Incarnation," pp. 193–97; Kosambi, "Avatāra Syncretism"; also Otto Schrader, *Introduction to the Pāñcarātra and the Ahirbudhnya Saṁhitā* (Madras: Adyar Library, 1916), pp. 35–59.

19. Cf. Edward C. Dimock, Jr., *The Place of the Hidden Moon* (Chicago: University of Chicago Press, 1966), pp. 192–95.

20. See the glossary in the clothbound edition, s.v. *adbhuta, śṛṅgāra.*

21. Cf. *Matsya P.* I.29 ff.; *Bhāgavata P.* VIII.24. See Hopkins, *Epic Mythology,* pp. 201–2.

22. Cf. *Gītagovinda* I.23; *Mahābhārata* I.16.10–11; *Bhāgavata P.* XII.13.2. See Gonda, *Aspects of Viṣṇuism,* pp. 126–29; Klaus Rüping, *Amṛtamanthana und Kūrma-Avatāra* (Weisbaden: Harrassowitz, 1970).

23. Cf. *Atharva Veda* XII.1.48 (*sūḳara*); *Viṣṇu P.* V.29.23 (*śūḳara*); *Bhāgavata P.*

4 Krishna: Cosmic Cowherd Lover (cont.)

III.18–19 (śūkara). See Gonda, Aspects of Viṣṇuism, pp. 129–45; V. S. Agrawala, Solar Symbolism of the Boar: Yajña-varāha—An Interpretation (Varanasi: Prithivi Prakashan, 1963).

24. Cf. Viṣṇu P. I.17–21; Bhāgavata P. VII.2–8.

25. See Ṛg Veda I.154.1–6, 155.3–5; Śatapatha Brāhmaṇa I.9.3.8 ff.; Gonda, Aspects of Viṣṇuism, pp. 55–72, 145–46; F.B.J. Kuiper, "The Three Strides of Viṣṇu," in Indological Studies in Honor of W. Norman Brown (New Haven: American Oriental Society, 1962), pp. 137–51; Wendy O'Flaherty, Hindu Myths (London: Penguin, 1975), Bibliographical Notes, pp. 328–29.

26. See Bhāgavata P. VIII.19–23.

27. See Mahābhārata III.115–17; Bhāgavata P. IX.15–17; Hopkins, Epic Mythology, pp. 184, 211.

28. See Bhāgavata P. IX.10–11.

29. See Mahābhārata I.189.31; Viṣṇu P. V.1.59–63.

30. See Viṣṇu P. V.25; Bhāgavata P. X.65; Hopkins, Epic Mythology, p. 212.

31. See, e.g., Matsya P. 47.247; and Agni Purāṇa, Ānandāśrama Sanskrit Series, no. 41 (Poona: Ānandāśrama Press, 1900) ch. 16; cf. Bhāgavata P. I.3.24; Sastri, "Pallava Statues," pp. 5–7.

32. See Dimock, Hidden Moon, pp. 26–29.

33. See Mahābhārata III.188–89; Bhāgavata P. I.3.25; Gonda, Aspects of Viṣṇuism, pp. 149–50.

34. See Harivaṁśa 50–64; Viṣṇu P. V.6–14; Bhāgavata P. X.5–37; Bālacarita in Plays Ascribed to Bhāsa, edited by C. R. Devadhar (Poona: Oriental Book Agency, 1962), pp. 511–60. See also Gonda, Aspects of Viṣṇuism, pp. 154–64; Ruben, Krishna, pp. 45 ff.

35. The more common reading of the refrain as jaya jaya deva hare ignores the word play and the significance of Jayadeva as an epithet.

36. A reference to the Mahābhārata as jaya, which comes at the beginning of the epic (I.1.1), may not be relevant to the meaning of Jayadeva's signature and his epithet for Krishna, but it seems worth noting:

नारायणं namaskṛtya naraṁ caiva narottamam |
devīṁ sarasvatīṁ caiva tato jayam udīrayet ||

37. See Hopkins, Epic Mythology, pp. 215, 217.

38. See Mahābhārata III.194.15; Harivaṁśa 52.2; Bhāgavata P. VIII.17.4; X.32.2.

39. See Harivaṁśa 52.4.

40. See Pāṇini, Aṣṭādhyāyī III.1.138, vārt. 2: gāvādiṣu vinde saṁjñāyas. In the form of Varāha, the Boar, Govinda is gāṁ vindatṛ, "finder of earth"; Mahābhārata I.19.11.

41. See Mahābhārata I.59.22.

42. See Mahābhārata II.13.33, V.126.37f.; Harivaṁśa 27, 44–48, 65–78; Bhāgavata P. X.1–4, 36–44.

43. See Ruben, Krishna, pp. 107–8.

———•••———

Introduction 54

44. See, e.g., *Mahābhārata* I.15; Hopkins, *Epic Mythology*, pp. 206, 208, 213–14.

45. Discussed in section 3; cf. *Harivaṁśa* 49; *Viṣṇu P.* 6.4 ff.; *Bhāgavanta P.* X .5.1 ff.

46. See *Mahābhārata* I.31.10; *Harivaṁśa* 55–56; *Bhāgavata P.* X.16–17.

47. See *Harivaṁśa* 50.20–23.

48. See *Mahābhārata* I.20–30; Gonda, *Aspects of Viṣṇuism*, pp. 101–3.

49. See Ruben, *Krishna*, pp. 112 ff.

50. See, e.g., Lévi-Strauss, *Honey to Ashes;* Yolanda and Robert Murphy, *Women of the Forest* (New York: Columbia University Press, 1975).

51. The Jumna has its confluence with the Ganges at Allahabad. It flows through Brindaban. It is also called *Kālindanandinī* (*GG* III.2), "daughter of Mt. Kalinda." Cf. *Harivaṁśa* 55.27 ff.

52. Cf. *Harivaṁśa* 63.18–35; *Viṣṇu P.* V.13.47–55; *Bhāgavata P.* III.2.14; X.33; *Bālacarita* III.1–3. See V. Raghavan, *Bhoja's Śṛṅgāra Prakāśa* (Madras: Punarvasu, 1963), pp. 561–73.

53. See O'Flaherty, *Mythology of Śiva*, pp. 141–72; also the glossary in the clothbound edition of this book, s.v. *anaṅga, kāma, rati,* and related references.

54. See the glossary in the clothbound edition of this book, s.v. *kānta, dayita, priya.*

55. Cf. *Bhāgavata P.* VII.20.3. Also *kaitava,* "deceitful," *GG* VIII.2*; cf. *Kumārasaṁbhava,* edited by Suryakanta (New Delhi: Sahitya Akademi, 1962), VIII.3.

56. This is given as a way to angrily address a *nāyaka;* see *Nāṭyaśāstra,* XXIV.310.

5 Rādhā: Consort of Krishna's Springtime Passion

1. Much of this material has been published in a more technical form in an article entitled, "Rādhā: Consort of Krishna's Vernal Passion," *Journal of the American Oriental Society,* 95, no. 4 (1975), 655–71.

In my attempt to describe the nature of Rādhā's relation to Krishna in literature antedating the *Gītagovinda,* I have drawn on the work of several scholars. See Śaśibhuṣan Dasgupta, *Śrīrādhār kramabikāśa—darśane o sāhitye* (Calcutta: E. Mukherji, 1953, B.S. 1359); A. K. Majumdar, "A Note on the Development of the Rādhā Cult," *Annals of the Bhandarkar Institute,* 36 (1955), pp. 231–57; Harekrishna Mukhopādhyāya, *Kavijayadeva śrīgītagovinda* (Calcutta: Gurudās Mukhopādhyāy, 1956, B.S. 1362); B. Majumdar, *Kṛṣṇa in History and Legend* (Calcutta: University of Calcutta, 1969), pp. 165–232; S. L. Katre, "Kṛṣṇa, Gopas, Gopīs, and Rādhā," in *P. K. Gode Commemoration Volume,* edited by H. L. Hariyappa and M. M. Patkar (Poona: Oriental Book Agency, 1960), pp. 83–92. In the Vaishnava literature that postdates the *Gītagovinda,* Rādhā is a ubiquitous figure in relation to Krishna; since some excellent studies of these works exist, I do not deal with the material here. See Shashibhusan Dasgupta, *Obscure Religious Cults* (Calcutta: K. L. Mukhopadhyay, 1962), pp. 113–46; S. K. De, *Vaiṣṇava Faith and Movement in Bengal* (Calcutta: K. L. Mukhopadhyay, 1961); Edward C. Dimock, Jr., *The Place of the Hidden Moon: Erotic Mysticism in the Vaishnava Sahajiyā Cult of Bengal* (Chicago: University of Chicago Press, 1966); Norvin Hein, *The Miracle Plays of Mathurā* (New Haven: Yale University Press, 1972), pp. 163–271; Milton Singer, ed., *Krishna: Myths, Rites and Attitudes* (Honolulu: East-West Center Press, 1966). I have also

5 Rādhā: Consort of Krishna's Springtime Passion (cont.)

omitted references from two works that make some claim for inclusion. Original verses on Rādhā quoted in *Saduktikarṇāmṛta* (edited by S. K. Banerji; Calcutta: K. L. Mukhopadhyay, 1965) are attributed to Jayadeva's contemporaries Umāpatidhara and Śaraṇa (I.53.5, I.55.3, I.61.2); another (I.58.4) is quoted below from *Vakroktijīvita* (2.56). Verses on Rādhā in the *Kṛṣṇakarṇāmṛta* of Līlāśuka Bilvamaṅgala are numerous, but the dating of the work remains problematic (it is variously assigned to periods ranging from the ninth to the fifteenth century). See S. K. De, *The Kṛṣṇā-karṇāmṛta*, University of Dacca Oriental Publication Series, no. 5 (Dacca: University of Dacca, 1938), Francis Wilson, *The Love of Krishna: The Kṛṣṇakarṇāmṛta of Līlāśuka Bilvamaṅgala* (Philadelphia: University of Pennsylvania Press, 1975).

2. H. Grassman, *Wörterbuch zum Rig-Veda* (1872; reprint, Wiesbaden: Otto Harrassowitz, 1955), 1160–62; *Bhāgavata Purāṇa* (Gorakhpur: Gita Press, 1962) II.4.14; IV.7.57, 24.18, 31.11; IX.21.17; X.65.6.

3. Max Müller, ed., *The Hymns of the Rig-Veda*, 2 vols. (London: Trübner, 1877) VIII.61.14; cf. I.30.5, etc; related epithets *vasupati, vasudā,* etc.

4. See J. Gonda, *Aspects of Early Viṣṇuism* (1954; reprint, Delhi: Motilal Banarsidass, 1969), pp. 224–25; see also *The Mahābhārata*, critical edition, edited by V. S. Sukthankar, et al. (Poona: Bhandarkar Oriental Research Institute, 1933–36), I:16.

5. E.g., R. C. Artal, "A Note on Kṛṣṇa and His Consort Rādhā," *Anthropological Society of Bombay*, 8, no. 5 (1907–9), 356–60; Sukumar Sen, "Etymology of the Name Rādhā," *Indian Linguistics*, 8 (1943), 434. Sen speculates that the word *rādhā* must have been a common noun with the meaning of "beloved, desired woman." He supports his argument with reference to the Vedic *rādhas* meaning "a desired object" and its masculine cognate in Avestan *rāδa*, meaning "lover" in Yasna 9.23. My colleague Professor Dale Bishop informs me that the passage is problematic, but if it is taken with a Gāthic passage (Yasna 29.9) where the only other reference to *rāδa* occurs, the contexts suggest that the word could mean something like "satisfaction" as an abstract; in any case, most scholarly interpretations indicate something or someone that "fulfills a need."

6. A. A. Macdonell and A. B. Keith, *Vedic Index* (1912, reprint, Delhi: Motilal Banarsidass, 1967), vol. I, p. 417. *Atharva Veda* XIX.7.3(c–d):

rādhe viśākhe suhávānurādhā   jyéṣṭā sunákṣatram ariṣṭaṁ múlam ||

Atharvaveda Saṁhitā, edited by W. D. Whitney and R. Roth (Berlin: F. Dummler, 1856), p. 356. Although Whitney reports all manuscripts examined to read *rādhe* (fem. dual) and commentaries to explain this as meaning that *rādhā* is another name for *viśākhā*, he feels that it is an interpolation based on a later misunderstanding of *anurādhā* as meaning "the one after (*anu*) or following *rādhā*." He therefore changes the reading to *rādho* and translates it "be the two Viśākhās bestowal (*rādhas*)." W. D. Whitney, trans., *Atharva-veda Saṁhitā* (1905; reprint, Delhi: Motilal Banarsidass, 1962), vol. II, p. 908. If one follows the manuscript evidence and reads *rādhe,* it can be understood that the two stars called *Viśākhā* are identified with a dual *rādhā.* The identification is supported by the fifth century lexical work *Amarakoṣa*, I.3.22: *rādhā viśākhā puṣye tu sidhyatiṣyau śraviṣṭhayā,* etc. Amarasiṁha, *The Nāmaliṅgānuśāsanam* (*Amarakoṣa*), edited by Pandit Śivadatta (Bombay: Nirṇayasāgara Press, 1944), p. 38.

7. Rajendra Mittra, ed., Taittirīya Brāhmaṇa Bibliotheca Indica, no. 125 (Calcutta: Asiatic Society of Bengal, 1855), p. 4.

8. *Taittirīya Saṁhitā,* translated by A. B. Keith, Harvard Oriental Series, vols. 18–19 (Cambridge, Mass.: Harvard University Press, 1914).

9. *Mahābhārata* XIII.135.60(c), *nakṣatranemir nakṣatrī;* in the episode of the burning of Khāṇḍava forest (I.214 ff.) Krishna is repeatedly addressed as *Mādhava,* and also *Madhusūdana;* see section 4, notes 9–12 above, esp. Gonda, *Aspects of Viṣṇuism,* pp. 16 ff., 237.

10. F. E. Pargiter, *Ancient Indian Historical Tradition* (London: Oxford University Press, 1922), p. 135.

11. *Amaraḳoṣa,* I.3.22; the authors of the *Brahmavaivarta P.* incorporate Rādhā's *nakṣatrā* associations into the story of her heavenly birth and descent; see Walter Ruben, "The Kṛṣṇacarita in the Harivaṁśa and Certain Purāṇas," *Journal of the American Oriental Society,* 61 (1941), 126–27.

12. This Rādhā has no apparent connection with the epic figure named Rādhā, who is the wife of the charioteer Adhiratha and the foster-mother of Kunti's son Karṇa. *Mahābhārata* I.104.14(b) and 181.28(a):

> *tam utsṛṣṭaṁ tadā garbhaṁ rādhābhartā mahāyaśaḥ* |
> *putratve ḳalpayāmāsa sabhāryaḥ sūtanandaḥ* ||

Rādhā's renowned husband [Adhiratha], son of a charioteer,
Rescued the abandoned child and he and his wife made him their own son.

> *ḳo hi rādhāsutaṁ ḳarṇaṁ śaḳto yodhayituṁ raṇe* |
> *anyatra rāmād droṇād vā ḳrpād vāpi śaradvataḥ* ||

Who can fight in battle with Rādhā's son Karṇa
Other than Paraśurāma, Droṇa, Kṛpa, or Śaradvat?

13. See Dimock, *Place of the Hidden Moon,* pp. 32–35; B. Majumdar, *Kṛṣṇa in History and Legend,* pp. 171–91.

14. References to Rādhā in these Purāṇas are given in tentative chronological order.

Matsya Purāṇa, edited by H. N. Apte, Ānandāśrama Sanskrit Series, no. 54 (Poona: Ānandāśrama Press, 1907), XIII.38. In verses 24–53 of this section, Devī ennumerates her various names at different holy places in response to Dakṣa's question as to what names are to be invoked at the *tīrthas.* Verse 38 is quoted by Jīva Gosvāmin in his commentary on *Bhāgavata* X.21.17.

> *śivakuṇḍe śivānandā nandinī deviḳātaṭe* |
> *rukmiṇī dvāravatyāṁ tu rādhā vṛndāvane vane* || 38 ||

At Śivakuṇḍa she is Śivānandā; at Devikātaṭe she is Nandinī;
At Dvāravatī she is Rukmiṇī; in the forest at Vṛndāvana she is Rādhā.

Liṅga Purāṇa, edited by P. J. Vidyasagara (Calcutta: Valmiki Press, 1885), Uttarārdhe 48.14. The verse is one of a series of mantras (48.5–26) in imitation of the Gāyatrī, all ending *pracodayāt,* in which various gods and goddesses are invoked; 48.12 invokes Vishnu, 48.13 Lakṣmī.

> *samuddhṛtāyai vidmahe viṣṇunaiḳena dhīmahi* |
> *tan no rādhā pracodayāt* || 14 ||

We know about one whom Vishnu himself redeems, we meditate on her—
Then let Rādhā inspire us!

5 Rādhā: Consort of Krishna's Springtime Passion (cont.)

Varāha Purāṇa, edited by Hrshikeśa Śāstrī, Bibliotheca Indica, no. 109 (Calcutta: Asiatic Society of Bengal, 1887), 164.33–35. Krishna's encounter with Rādhā here follows his slaying of the demon Ariṣṭa. Note that Ariṣṭa appears in apposition to the nakṣatra Mūla in the Atharva Veda passage quoted above in note 7.

tatra rādhā samāśliṣya kṛṣṇam akliṣṭakāraṇam |
svanāmnā viditaṁ kuṇḍaṁ kṛtaṁ tīrtham adūrataḥ || 33 ||
rādhākuṇḍam iti khyātaṁ sarvapāpaharaṁ śubham |
ariṣṭarādhākuṇḍābhyāṁ snānāt phalam avāpnuyāt |
rājasūyāśvamedhānāṁ nātra kāryyā vicāraṇā |
gohatyābrahmahatyāyāḥ pāpaṁ kṣipraṁ vinaśyati || 34|35 ||

Since Rādhā embraced tireless Krishna there,
The tank was known by her name and a holy place was created nearby.
It was known as "Rādhā's tank," removing all sins, auspicious.
With ablution from the Ariṣṭa tank and the Rādhā tank
One may doubtless attain the reward of Rājasūya and Aśvamedha rites—
It quickly destroys the sin of cow killing and even Brahman killing.

Brahmavaivarta Purāṇa, edited by V. G. Apte, Ānandāśrama Sanskrit Series, no. 102 (Poona: Ānandāśrama Press, 1935), translated by Rajendra Nath Sen, Sacred Books of the Hindus, vol. 24 (Allahabad: Pāṇini Office, 1922); Kṛṣṇa-janma-khaṇḍa, adhyāyas 2–5, 15, 17, 27–30, 52, 53, 57, 58, 66–68, 92–98, 110, 111, 123–28. Rādhā occupies a leading position in the section devoted to Krishna's birth. This elaborate section seems to be as late as the sixteenth century in its present form, but since it is an obvious compilation of various strands of the Rādhā legend it furnishes many relevant suggestions about the nature of the figure and her relationship to Krishna. See Cheever MacKenzie Brown, God as Mother: A Feminine Theology in India (Hartford, Vt.: Claude Stark, 1974).

An older version of this Purāṇa may be as early as the eighth century; see A. J. Rawal, "Some Problems Regarding the Brahmavaivartapurāṇa," Purāṇa, 14, no. 2 (1972), 107–24.

Padma Purāṇa, edited with Hindi paraphrase by S. S. Śarma (Bareli: Saṁskrtisamsthāna, 1968); Pātāla-khaṇḍa (IV), 52, Śrīrādhā-janmāṣṭami-mahātmya. This section is noted several times in the attempts of the Gosvāmins to fix Rādhā's place in established textual traditions, but the section itself seems to me to be a crude interpolation aimed at elevating Rādhā's position in a more orthodox Vishnu cult. Rādhā's lowly birth as a cowherdess is rationalized by explaining that she is called gopī ("cow-protectress") because she conserves energy; she is one of the chief deities, the hlādinī-śakti of Krishna; she is Mahālakṣmī and Krishna Nārāyaṇa, etc. The Gosvāmin commentators quote this with reference to Kārttikamahātmya, of Pātāla-khaṇḍa; see A. K. Majumdar, "Note on the Rādhā Cult," pp. 245–46.

For discussions of Purāṇic chronology, see A. D. Pusalker, Studies in the Epics and Purāṇas (Bombay: Bharatiya Vidya Bhavan, 1963), pp. 205–30; R. C. Hazra, "Studies in the Purāṇic Records on Hindu Rites and Customs," University of Dacca Bulletin, no. 20 (Dacca, 1940); M. Winternitz, Geschichte der indischen Litterature (Leipzig: C. F. Amelangs Verlag, 1909), vol. I, pp. 440–83. In The Purana Index (Madras: University of Madras, 1951–55) under "Rādhā" V.R.R. Dikshitar lists additional references to Rādhā in Brahmāṇḍa Purāṇa (III.36.56; 42.21, 47–48; 43.21 and 29; 44.29) and Vāyu Purāṇa (105.52), but these could not be located in editions available to me. The late date and derivative nature of treatments of Rādhā in *Devībhāgavata* (translated by Swami Vijñānanda in Sacred Books of the Hindus, vol. 23; Allahabad: Pāṇini Office, 1922, chapter IX, pp. 797–1008) and *Mahābhāgavata* (edited by M. I. Desai; Bombay: Gujarati Printing Press, 1913) has made me omit them from the list; see A. K. Majumdar, "Note on the Rādhā Cult," pp. 246–47; also, R. D. Hazra, "The Mahābhāgavata-purāṇa," *Indian Historical Quarterly,* 28 (1952), 17–28.

15. *Bhāgavata Purāṇa* (Gita Press edition) X.30.28:

> anayārādhito nūnam bhāgavan harir īśvaraḥ |
> yan no vihāya govindaḥ prīto yām anayad rahaḥ ||

> Lord Hari, God, was certainly satisfied by her—
> For, leaving us, Govinda, the lover, led her in secret.

16. *Bhāgavata Purāṇa,* Murshidabad edition, with the commentaries of Śrīdhara-svāmin, Sanātana Gosvamin, Jīva Gosvāmin, and Viśvanātha Cakravartī (Berhampur: Rādhāraman Press, 1888, B.S. 1294). Later commentators identify the figure of the solitary *gopī* with *hlādinī-śakti,* the means by which Krishna gives bliss to his devotees; see Dimock, *Place of the Hidden Moon,* pp. 134, 203–4. It is worth noting again that in the *Bhāgavata,* the *rāsa* dance is an autumnal rite where the emphasis is on Krishna's ability to love all the cowherdesses simultaneously, whereas Krishna's love with Rādhā is an erotic duet enacted in springtime. Following the *Bhāgavata* identification, other commentators claim reference to Rādhā in similar passages in other texts, e.g., *Harivaṁśa,* critical edition, edited by P. L. Vaidya (Poona: Bhandarkar Oriental Research Institute, 1969), 6.33:

> hāheti kurvatas tasya prahṛṣṭās tā varāṅganāḥ |
> jagṛhur nihsṛtāṁ vāṇiṁ sāmnā dāmodareritām ||

The seventeenth-century Maharastrian commentator Nīlakaṇṭha explains the verse as Krishna's call for Rādhā; see the edition of R. Kinjawadekar (Poona: Citraśāla Press, 1936), II.20.33. Also, *Viṣṇu Purāṇa* (Gorakhpur: Gita Press, 1962) V.13.33–46; commenting on *Bhāgavata* X.32.8, Sanātana Gosvāmin refers to this passage.

17. Charlotte Vaudeville, "Evolution of Love-Symbolism in Bhagavatism," *Journal of the American Oriental Society,* 82 (1962), 31–40; see also Jean Filliozat, "Les Dates du Bhāgavatapurāṇa et du Bhāgavatamāhātmya," in *Indological Studies in Honor of W. Norman Brown,* American Oriental Series, vol. 47 (New Haven; American Oriental Society, 1962), pp. 70–77; Thomas J. Hopkins, The Social Teaching of the *Bhāgavata Purāṇa,*" and J.A.B. van Buitenen, "On the Archaism of the *Bhāgavata Purāṇa,*" in Milton Singer, ed., *Krishna: Myths, Rites, and Attitudes* (Honolulu: East-West Center, 1966), pp. 3–40.

18. The *Harivaṁśa* episode of Krishna's marriage to Nīlā is not known in the Northern Recension and is given by Vaidya as Appendix I, no. 12. Local traditions contribute many variants to events and figures in the Krishna story; see Walter Ruben, *Krishna: Konkordanz und Kommentar der Motive Seines Heldenlebens,* Istanbuler Schriften, no. 17 (Istanbul, 1944).

19. See J.S.M. Hooper, *Hymns of the Ālvārs* (Calcutta: Association Press, 1929), pp. 55, 62; V.V.R. Dikshitar, *Śilappadikāram* (London: Oxford University Press, 1939), p. 229.

20. Occurrences of the name Rādhā in prose portions of *Lalitavistara* (*tena khalu punar bhikṣavaḥ samayena sujātāyā grāmikaduhiturdāsī rādhā nāma kālagatābhūt),*

5 Rādhā: Consort of Krishna's Springtime Passion (cont.)

edited by P. L. Vaidya (Darbhanga, 1958) and the vulgate of *Pañcatantra* (*kim param tu rādhā nāma me bhāryā gopakulaprasūtā prathamam āsīt sā tvam atrāvatīrṇā*) edited by K. P. Parab (Bombay: Nirṇayasāgara Press, 1950, p. 54) are difficult to date.

21. On dating, see A. B. Keith, *History of Sanskrit Literature* (1920; reprint, London: Oxford University Press, 1956), pp. 223–24. For *Sattasaī*, see vulgate, entitled *Gāthasaptaśatī*, edited with the commentary of Gaṅgādharabhatta by P. Durgāprasād and K. P. Parab, Kāvyamālā, no. 21 (Bombay: Nirṇayasāgara Press, 1933), I.89; and critical text, *Saptaśatakam des Hāla*, edited with German translation by Albrecht Weber, *Abhandlungen für die Kunde des Morgenländes*, 5, no. 3 (1870; reprint, Nendeln, Liechtenstein: Kraus Reprint, 1966), I.86:

> *muhamāruena taṁ kaṇha goraaṁ rāhiāĕ avaṇento |*
> *etāṇaṁ vallaviṇaṁ annānaṁ vi goraaṁ harasi ||* I.89 (Weber I.86) ||

The Sanskrit version would be:

> *mukhamārutena tvaṁ kṛṣṇa gorajo rādhikāyā apanayan |*
> *etāsāṁ ballavīnām anyāsām api gauravaṁ harasi ||*

In another verse (2.28; Weber, 131) an unnamed *gopī* is singled out and associated with singing and spring; the alliterative pattern of the verse also makes it relevant to *Gītagovinda*.

> *mahumāsamāruāhaamahuarajhaṁkāraṇibbhare raṇṇe |*
> *gāaī virahakkharavaddhapahiamaṇamohaṇaṁ govī ||*

"In woods full of humming bees attacked by winds of the honeyed month of spring, a *gopī* sings a seductive chant to bind a traveler's heart with words of her neglected love."

22. Dated according to the dating of Vākpati's patron, Yaśovarma of Kanauj, by Kalhaṇa in the *Rājataraṅginī*. *Gaüḍavaho: A Historical Poem in Prākṛt*, edited by S. P. Pandit, Bombay Sanskrit Series, no. 34 (Bombay: Central Book Depot, 1887), v. 22:

> *ṇaha-rehā rāhā-kāraṇā oṁ karuṇaṁ harantu vo sarasā |*
> *vaccha-tthalammi kotthuha-kiraṇāantī oṁ kaṇhassa ||*

Pandit's Sanskrit version reads *nakharekhā rādhākaraṇā* (*rādhayā gopyā nirmitāḥ karajaprahārāḥ*) *karuṇānimittaṁ* (*saṁsāraduḥkhaṁ*) *harantu* (*nāśayantu*) *sarasā* (*ārdrā*) *vakṣaḥsthale kaustubhakiraṇāyamānāḥ kṛṣṇasya*.

23. Bhaṭṭa Nārāyaṇa is dated to the first half of the seventh century by D. D. Kosambi in his introduction to *Subhāṣitaratnakoṣa*, edited by Kosambi and V. V. Gokhale, Harvard Oriental Series, no. 42 (Cambridge, Mass: Harvard University Press, 1957), p. lxxxiii, but the only basis for dating is the citations to his work by Vāmana and Ānandavardhana, which places him before the ninth century; see A. B. Keith, *The Sanskrit Drama* (1924, reprint London: Oxford University Press, 1959), p. 212.

Veṇīsaṁhāra of Bhaṭṭa Nārāyaṇa, edited by Julius Grill (Leipzig: Fues's Verlag, 1871), *nāndī* 2:

kālindyāḥ pulineṣu kelikupitām utsrjya rāse rasaṁ
  gacchantīm anugacchato 'srukaluṣāṁ kaṁsadviṣo rādhikām |
tatpādapratimāniveśitapadasyodbhūtaromodgater
  akṣuṇṇo'nunayaḥ prasannadayitādrṣṭasya puṣṇātu vaḥ ||

This *nāndī*, like the two others accompanying it in most editions, could have been added to the text at any time, but the subject of Rādhā's sulking and Krishna's pacifying her is sufficiently relevant to the theme of Draupadī's insults and Bhīma's soothing her with revenge to be part of the original play. It is noteworthy too that after the three *nāndī* verses, the *sūtradhāra* goes on to praise Vishnu and to inform the audience that Krishna has undertaken to act as mediator between the Kauravas and Pāṇḍavas.

24. *Dhvanyāloka* of Ānandavardhana, edited, with the commentary of Abhinavagupta, by P. Durgāprasād and K. P. Parab, Kāvyamālā, no. 25 (Bombay: Nirṇayasāgara Press, 1891), 2.6, 3.41, critical text and translation by K. Krishnamoorthy (Dharwar: Karnatak University, 1974), 2.5, 3.40.

teṣāṁ gopavadhūvilāsasuhrdāṁ rādhārahahsākṣiṇām
  kṣemaṁ bhadra kalindaśailatanayātīre latāveśmanām |
vicchinne smaratalpakalpanamrducchedopayoge 'dhunā
  te jāne jaraṭhībhavanti vigalannīlatviṣaḥ pallavāḥ || 2.6 ||

This verse is attributed to the poetess Vidyā in the *Subhāṣitaratnakoṣa* (808). The translation and all others from Vidyākara's anthology cited here are by Daniel H. H. Ingalls, quoted from his *Sanskrit Court Poetry*, Harvard Oriental Series, vol. 44 (Cambridge, Mass.: Harvard University Press, 1965).

durārādhā rādhā subhaga yad anenāpi mrjatas
  tavaitat prāṇeśājaghanavasanenāśru patitam |
kaṭhoraṁ strīcetas tad alam upacārair virama he
  kriyāt kalyāṇaṁ vo harir anunayeṣu evam uditaḥ || 3.41 ||

It seems significant that Ānandavardhana is the earliest writer to illustrate his theories with examples from existing Sanskrit and Prākrit literature rather than composing his own. Abhinavagupta, in commenting on these two verses, attributes the first to Krishna after he has left Mathurā for Dvārakā; he says the second is Rādhā's words to Krishna.

25. *Dhvanyālokalocana* of Abhinavagupta, commentary on the two *Dhvanyāloka* verses quoted in note 24; another reference to Rādhā quoted in the *Locana* on 1.4 (Kāvyamālā ed., p. 25).

yāte dvāravatīṁ tadā madhuripau taddattakampānatāṁ
  kālindītaṭarūḍhavañjulalatām āliṅgya sotkanṭhayā |
tadgītaṁ gurubāṣpagadgadagalattārasvaraṁ rādhayā
  yenāntarjalacāribhir jalacarair apy utkam utkūjitam ||

V. Raghavan notes that in his *Abhinavabhāratī;* Abhinavagupta quotes from a work, now lost, entitled *Rādhāvipralambha;* Bhoja categorizes the work as a *rāsakāṅka.* See V. Raghavan, *Bhoja's Śṛṅgāra Prakāśa* (Madras: Punarvasu, 1963), p. 567; idem., "Writers Quoted in the Abhinavabhāratī," *Journal of Oriental Research, Madras,* 6 (1932).
  See also the *Vakroktijīvita* of Kuntaka, dated mid tenth to eleventh century (edited by S. K. De, 3d ed.; Calcutta: K. L. Mukhopadhyay, 1961), chapters 1–3.

5 Rādhā: Consort of Krishna's Springtime Passion (cont.)

The verse *teṣāṁ gopavadhūo*, quoted from *Dhvanyāloka* (2.6), is cited illustratively in the *svopajñavṛtti* on 3.3–4; the verse *yāte dvaravatīm*, quoted from the *Locana*, is cited in the *svopajñavṛtti* on 2.59, with the variants (a) *taddattasaṁpādanāṁ* (b) *kālindījalakelivañjulalatām ālambya*.

26. *Kāvyamīmāṁsa* of Rājaśekhara, edited by C. D. Dalal and R. A. Shastry, Gaekwad's Oriental Series, no. 1 (Baroda: Central Library, 1916), p. 71. Two verses comparing the breaths of Śiva and Hari are quoted in *adhyāya* 13 following the comment *atha tulyadehitulyasya bhidāḥ. . . . tasyaiva vastuno viṣayāntarayojanād anyarūpāpattir viṣayaparivartaḥ.*

> *ye sīmantitagātrabhasmarajaso ye kumbhakadveṣiṇo*
> *ye līḍhāḥ śravaṇāśrayeṇa phaniṇā ye candraśaityadruhaḥ |*
> *te kupyadgirijāvibhaktavapuṣaś cittavyathāsākṣiṇaḥ*
> *sthānor dakṣiṇanāsikāpuṭabhuvaḥ śvāsānilāḥ pāntu vaḥ ||*
> *ye kirṇakvathitodarābjamadhavo ye mlāpitorahsrajo*
> *ye tāpāt taralena talpaphaṇinā pītapratāpojjhitāḥ |*
> *te rādhāsmṛtisākṣiṇaḥ kamalayā sāsūyam ākarṇitā*
> *gāḍhāntardavathoḥ prataptasaralāḥ śvāsā hareḥ pāntu vaḥ ||*

See *Subhāṣitaratnakoṣa* 136, with variants.

27. *Damayantīkathā* is the oldest extant *campū-kāvya;* Keith, *History of Sanskrit Literature*, pp. 332–33. *Damayantīkathā* (also called *Nalacampū*) of Trivikrama Bhaṭṭa, edited by N. B. Parvaṇīkar, P. Durgāprasād, and P. Śivadatta, with the commentary of Caṇḍapāla (Bombay: Nirṇayasāgara Press, 1931), p. 108 (chapter 4).

> *kevalam anavarataśikṣitavaidagdhyakalāparādhātmikātrapāparihṛtya guṇino*
> *gurūn parapuruṣe māyāvini kṛtakeśivadhe dhṛtamandarāge rāgaṁ badhnāti |*

The sense of this passage is based on a series of puns: "She being not very much taught [or, "not newly taught in sexual pleasures"] in the arts of cunning [or, "passion"] and committing a fault of giving up modesty [*aparādhā-ātmika; rādhā-ātmikā* means "as Radha did"], ignoring the virtuous elders, set her passion on the highest man [or, "a stranger, other than her husband"], Krishna [*māyāvin* also means "trickster"], slayer of demon Keśi [*kṛta-keśi-vadhe; kṛtake 'śivadhe* means "who is artificial, who confers evil"], upholder of Mt. Mandara [or, "whose passion was inactive"]."

For the *Yaśastilakacampūkāvya* the dating is firm; at the end of the text itself Somadeva says that he composed the work in *śāka* 881 (A.D. 959); verse from *Yaśastilakacampūkāvya* of Somadeva, edited, with the commentary of Śrutadeva Sūri, by M. P. Śivadatta and K. P. Parab, Kāvyamālā, no. 70 (Bombay: Nirṇayasāgara Press, 1903), p. 142. The example of Rādhā is cited in chapter 4, while the king is narrating the love of Amṛtamati:

> *tathā hi—purāpi kiṁ na reme gaṅgā saha maheśvareṇa, rādhā nārāyaṇena,*
> *bṛhaspatipatnī dvijarājena, tārā ca vālinā |*

See K. K. Handiqui, *Yaśastilaka and Indian Culture* (Sholapur: Jaina Samskṛti Samrakshaka Sangha, 1949), pp. 1–21.

28. Three copper-plate inscriptions of Vākpati-Muñja, dated v.s. 1031 (A.D. 974), v.s. 1038 (A.D. 982), v.s. 1043 (A.D. 986); v.s. 1031 plate: N. J. Kirtane, "On Three Mālwā Inscriptions," *Indian Antiquary*, 6 (1877), 48–53; v.s. 1038, 1043 plates: K. N.

Dikshit, "Three Copper-Plate Inscriptions from Gaonri," *Epigraphica Indica*, 23, no. 17, (1935), 108, 109, 112.

> *yal lakṣmīvadanendunā na sukhitaṁ yan nārdritaṁ vāridher*
> *vārā yan na nijena nābhisarasīpadmena śāntiṁ gatam |*
> *yac cheṣāhiphaṇāsahasramadhuraśvāsair na cāśvāsitaṁ*
> *tad rādhāvirahāturaṁ muraripor velladvapuḥ pātu vaḥ ||*

On the relation between Vākpati-Muñja and Bhoja, see Kirtane, pp. 49–50. Dikshit notes, "The most important information contained in these plates is regarding the migration of Brāhmaṇas from various parts of the country to Mālwā where they were recipients of donations at the hands of the Paramāra prince. In several instances the donees seem to have migrated all the way from Bengal. . . ." (p. 103).

29. *Sarasvatīkaṇṭhābharaṇa* of Bhoja, edited, with the commentary of Rāmasiṁha on I–III and of Jagaddhara on IV, by K. Durgāprasād and W. L. S. Pansikar, Kāvyamālā, no. 94 (Bombay: Nirṇayasāgara Press, 1934).

> *rātāvadyādhirājyā visarararasavidvyājavākkṣmāpakārā*
> *rākā pakṣmābhaśeṣā nayananayanasvā(sā)khayā stavyamārā |*
> *rāmā vyastasthiratvā tuhinananahituh śrīh karakṣāradhārā*
> *rādhā rakṣāstu mahyaṁ śivamamamavaśivyālavidyāvatārā || 2.294 ||*

> *kuśalaṁ rādhe sukhito 'si kaṁsa kaṁsaḥ kva nu sā rādhā |*
> *iti pārīprativacanair vilakṣahāso harir jayati || 2.351 ||*

> *kanakakalaśasvacche rādhāpayodharamaṇḍale*
> *navajaladharaśyāmām ātmadyvtiṁ pratibimbitām |*
> *asitasicayaprāntabhrāntyā muhur muhur utkṣipañ*
> *jayati janitavrīḍāhāsaḥ priyāhasito hariḥ || 3.110 ||*

This verse is cited again as 5.17; same as *Subhāṣitaratnakoṣa*, 147 (Kosambi and Gokhale ed., p. 29); Hemacandra's *Kāvyānuśāsana* 2.110, with variants (Parikh and Kulkarni ed. cited in note 31, p. 115).

> *gehād yātā saritam udakaṁ hārikā nājihīṣe*
> *maṅkṣyāmīti śrayasi yamunātīravīrudgrhāṇi |*
> *gosaṁdāyī viśasi vipināny eva govardhanādrer*
> *na tvaṁ rādhe dṛśi nipatitā devakīnandanasya || 4.177 ||*

> *līlāio ṇiasaṇe rakkhiu taṁ rāhiāi thaṇavaṭṭhe |*
> *hariṇo paḍhamasamāgamasajjhasavasarehiṁ veviro hattho || 5.235 ||*

The Sanskrit version reads: *līlāyito nivasane rakṣatu tvaṁ rādhikāyāḥ stanapṛṣṭhe | hareḥ prathamasamāgamasādhvasaprasarair vepanaśīlo hastaḥ ||*

> *pratyagrojjhitagokulasya śayanād utsvapnamūḍhasya me*
> *sā gotraskhalanād apaitu ca divā rādheti bhīror iti |*
> *rātrāv asvapato divā ca vijane lakṣmīti cābhyasyato*
> *rādhāṁ prasmarataḥ śriyam ramayataḥ khedo hareḥ pātu vaḥ || 5.448 ||*

> *helodastamahīdharasya tanutām ālokya doṣno harer*
> *hastenāṁsatate 'valambya caraṇāv āropya tatpādayoḥ |*
> *śailoddhārasahāyatām jigamiṣor aspṛṣṭagovardhanā*
> *rādhāyāḥ suciram jayanti gagane vandhyāḥ karabhrāntayaḥ || 5.493 ||*

30. *Daśāvatāracarita* by Kṣemendra, edited by P. Durgāprasād and K. P. Parab, Kāvyamālā, no. 26 (Bombay: Nirṇayasāgara Press, 1891), VIII.83, 170, 171, 176. Be-

5 Rādhā: Consort of Krishna's Springtime Passion (cont.)

cause the context seems important, the entire passage VIII.169–76 is quoted following VIII.83. It is this passage which Sukumar Sen considers to be the prototype of the *Gītagovinda;* see *History of Bengali Literature* (Delhi: Sāhitya Akademi, 1960), pp. 15–16.

prītyai babhūva kṛṣṇasya śyāmānicayacumbinaḥ |
jātī madhukarasyeva rādhevādhikavallabhā || 83 ||
tataḥ prabhāte saṁnaddhaṁ ratham āruhya sānugāḥ |
mathurāṁ yayur akrūrasaṁkarṣaṇajanārdanāḥ || 169 ||
kathaṁ rādhām anāmantryāgato 'ham iti mādhavaḥ |
aratiṁ mlānatāṁ cintāṁ vrajan bheje vinihśvasan || 170 ||
gacchan gokulagūḍhakuñjagahanāny ālokayan keśavaḥ
  sotkaṇṭhaṁ valitānano vanabhuvā sakhyeva ruddhāñcalaḥ |
rādhāyā na na neti nīviharaṇe vaiklavyalakṣyākṣarāh
  sasmāra smarasādhvasādbhutatano rāvokti[?]riktā giraḥ || 171 ||
govindasya gatasya kaṁsanagarīṁ vyāptā viyogāgninā
  snigdhaśyāmalakūlalīnahariṇī godāvarīgahvare[?] |
romanthasthitagoganaiḥ paricayād utkarṇam ākarṇitaṁ
  guptaṁ gokulapallave guṇaganaṁ gopyaḥ sarāgā jaguḥ || 172 ||
lalitavilāsakalāsukhakhelanalalanālobhanaśobhanayauvanamānitanavamadane |
alikulakokilakuvalayakajjalakālakalindasutāvivalajjalakāliyakuladamane |
keśikiśoramahāsuramāraṇadāruṇagokuladuritavidāraṇagovardhanadharaṇe |
kasya na nayanayugaṁ ratisajje majjati manasijataralataraṅge vararamaṇiramaṇe || 173 ||
udgīyamāne guṇasāgarasya guṇe guṇe rāgarasena śaureḥ |
gopāṅganā gūḍharasānurāgā muhur muhur mohahatā babhūvuḥ || 174 ||
govinde gurusaṁnidhau paravaśāveśād anuktvā gate
  suptānāṁ bakulasya śītalatale svairaṁ kuraṅgīdṛśām |
svapnāliṅganasaṁgate 'ṅgalatikāvikṣepalakṣyā muhur
  mugdhā vañcaka muñca muñca kitavety uccerur uccair giraḥ || 175 ||
rādhā mādhavaviprayogavigalajjīvopamānair muhur
  bāṣpaiḥ pīnapayodharāgragalitaiḥ phullatkadambākulā |
acchinnaśvasanena vegagatinā vyākīryamāṇaiḥ puraḥ
  sarvāśāpratibaddhamohamalinā prāvṛṇṇavevābhavat || 176 ||

31. *Subhāṣitaratnakoṣa* compiled by Vidyākara (cited in note 23). Verses 131; 136 = *Kāvyamimāṁsa* verse quoted above, with variants in the first and second *padas:* (a) *ye saṁtāpitanābhipadmamadhavo ye snāpitorahsrajo* (b) *prītapratīpojjhatāḥ*); 139; 147 = *Sarasvatīkaṇṭhābharaṇa* 3.11 quoted above, with variant in the fourth *pada:* (d) *janitavrīḍānamrapriyāhasito*); 808 = *Dhvanyāloka* 2.6 quoted above, with variants in the second and third *padas:* (b) *kalindarāja°,* (c) *smaratalpakalpana-vidhi°:* 980. Translations are by Ingalls, quoted from *Sanskrit Court Poetry.*

ete lakṣmaṇa jānakīvirahiṇaṁ māṁ khedayanty ambudā
  marmāṇīva ca ghaṭṭayanty alam amī krūrāḥ kadambānilāḥ |
itthaṁ vyāhṛtapūrvajanaviraho yo rādhayā vikṣitaḥ
  serṣyaṁ śaṅkitayā sa vaḥ sukhayatu svapnāyamāno hariḥ || 131 ||

agre gacchata dhenudugdokalaśānādāyagopye grhaṁ
  dugdhe vaskayaṇīkule punar iyaṁ rādhā śanair yāsyati |
ity anyavyapadeśaguptahṛdayaḥ kurvan viviktaṁ vrajaṁ
  devaḥ kāraṇanandasūnur aśivaṁ kṛṣṇaḥ sa muṣṇātu vaḥ || 139 ||

rathyākārpaṭikaih paṭaccaraśatasyūtorukanthābala-
pratyādiṣṭahimāgamārtiviśadaprasnigdhakaṇṭhodaraih |
gīyante nagareṣu nāgarajanapratyūṣanidrānudo
rādhāmādhavayoḥ paraspararahaḥprastāvanāgītayaḥ || 980 ||

Verse 980 is attributed to the Bengali poet Ḍimboka, who, like Jayadeva, is quoted in *Saduktikarṇāmṛta;* see D.H.H. Ingalls, "A Sanskrit Poetry of Village and Field: Yogeśvara and His Fellow Poets," *Journal of the American Oriental Society,* 74 (1954), 119–31.

32. Dated fourth quarter of the eleventh century, according to the dates of Vikramāditya VI, the Chalukya king whom Bilhaṇa served as *vidyāpati* and in whose honor *Vikramāṅkadevacarita* was composed. *Vikramāṅkadevacarita* of Bilhaṇa, edited by Georg Bühler, Bombay Sanskrit Series, no. 14 (Bombay: Central Book Depot, 1875), I.5, XVIII.87.

sāndrāṁ mudaṁ yacchatu nandako vaḥ sollāsalakṣmīpratibimbagarbhaḥ |
kurvann ajasraṁ yamunāpravāhasalīlarādhāsmaraṇaṁ murāreḥ || I.5 ||

dolāloladghanajaghanayā rādhayā yatra bhagnāḥ
kṛṣṇakrīḍāṅgaṇavitapino nādhunāpy ucchvasanti |
jalpakrīḍāmathitamathurāsūricakreṇa kecit
tasmin vṛndāvanaparisare vāsarā yena nītāḥ || XVIII.87 ||

See Barbara Stoler Miller, *Phantasies of a Love-Thief: The Caurapañcāśika Attributed to Bilhaṇa* (New York: Columbia University Press, 1971), pp. 188–91, which outline Bilhaṇa's travels.

33. In P. L. Vaidya, *Prakrit Grammar of Hemacandra, Revised Edition,* Bombay Sanskrit and Prakrit Series, no. 60 (Poona: Bhandarkar Oriental Research Institute, 1958), Appendix, pp. 190–91, 271–72; illustrative verses from Hemacandra are included in section describing characteristics of Apabhraṁśa: *adhyāya* 8, 4.420.2, 4.22.5.

hari naccāviu paṅgaṇai vimhai pāḍiu lou |
emvahiṁ rāha-paoharahaṁ jaṁ bhāvai taṁ hou || 4.420.2||

The Sanskrit version reads: *hariḥ nartitaḥ prāṅgane vismaye pātitaḥ lokaḥ | idānīṁ rādhāpayodharayoḥ yat (prati) bhāti tad bhavatu ||.*

ekamekvauṁ jai vi joedi hari suṭṭhu savvāyareṇa |
to vi drehi jahiṁ kahiṁ vi rāhī |
ko sakkai saṁvareṁ vi daḍḍha-nayaṇā nehiṁ paluṭṭā || 4.422.5||

The Sanskrit version reads: *ekaikaṁ yadyapi paśyati hariḥ suṣṭu sarvādareṇa | tathāpi dṛṣṭḥ yatra kvāpi rādhā | kaḥ śaknoti saṁvarītuṁ nayane snehena paryaste ||.*

In another work attributed to Hemacandra, the *Kāvyānuśāsana* (edited, with *Alaṁkāracūḍāmaṇi* and *Viveka,* by R. C. Parikh and V. M. Kulkarni; Bombay: Śrī Mahāvīra Jaina Vidyālaya, 1964), 2.8 (example 107) is the verse *teṣām gopavadhu°* . . . quoted from the *Dhvanyāloka,* 2.6; occurring also in *Vakroktijīvita,* 2.56 and *Subhāṣitaratnakoṣa,* 808; 2.11 (example 110) is the verse *kanakakalaśa°* quoted from *Sarasvatīkaṇṭhābharaṇa,* 3.110; 2.29 (example 131) is the verse *ete lakṣmaṇa* . . . quoted from *Subhāṣitaratnakoṣa,* 131.

34. *Naiṣadhīyacarita* of Śrīharṣa, edited, with the commentary of Nārāyaṇa, by P. Śivadatta and W.L.S. Pansikar (9th ed., Bombay: Nirṇayasāgara Press, 1952), 21.83.

5 *Rādhā: Consort of Krishna's Springtime Passion* (*cont.*)

praṇavatpraṇayirādha na rādhāputraśatrusakhitā sadṛśi te |
śrīpriyasya sadṛg eva tava śrīvatsam ātmahṛdi dhartum ajasram ||

35. Dated according to dating of Govardhana's patron Lakṣmaṇasena of Bengal (ca. A.D. 1185–1205); in *Gītagovinda* I.4, Jayadeva praises him for his erotic compositions. *Āryasaptaśatī* of Govardhana, edited, with the commentary of Anantapaṇḍita, by P. Durgāprasād and K. P. Parab, Kāvyamālā, no. 1 (Bombay: Nirṇayasāgara Press, 1886).

> *madhumathanamaulimāle sakhi tulayasi tulasi kiṁ mudhā rādhām |*
> *yat tava padam adasīyaṁ surabhayituṁ saurabhodbhedaḥ || 431 ||*
> *rājyābhiṣekasalilalakṣālitamauleḥ kathāsu kṛṣnasya |*
> *garvabharamantharākṣī paśyati padapaṅkajaṁ rādhā |*
> *lajjayitum akhilagopīnipītamanasaṁ madhudviṣaṁ rādhā |*
> *ajñeva pṛcchati kathāṁ śambhor dayitārdhatuṣṭasya || 508 ||*
> *lakṣmīnihsvāsānilapiṇḍīkṛtadugdhajaladhisārabhujaḥ |*
> *kṣīranidhitīrasudṛśo yaśāṁsi gāyanti rādhāyāḥ || 509 ||*
> *vicarati paritaḥ kṛṣṇe rādhāyaṁ rāgacapalanayanāyām |*
> *daśadigvedhaviśuddhaṁ viśikhaṁ vidadhāti viṣameṣuḥ || 530 ||*

36. Jayadeva certainy knew Kālidāsa's *Kumārasambhava*, and his conception of the significance of Rādhā's suffering may have been influenced by the image of Pārvatī's austerities preceding her union with Śiva.

37. *Caṇḍī* is also an epithet of Devī, the great goddess, with whom comparison is implied in the use of the term.

38. See Bharata's *Nāṭyaśāstra*, edited and translated by M. Ghosh (Calcutta: Granthalaya, 1967), XXIV.210–24; see also Dimock, *Place of the Hidden Moon,* pp. 215–20. Each state is defined in quotations from the *Nāṭyaśāstra* in the glossary to the Sanskrit text in the clothbound edition. The eighth of the classical states, that of a *proṣitabhartṛkā,* one whose lover is away in a distant place, is inappropriate to the context of the *Gītagovinda* and is not ascribed to Rādhā.

39. A detailed discussion of the significance of external manifestations of emotion in Indian esthetic theory is found in the introduction to my *Phantasies of a Love-Thief,* pp. 10–11.

40. *Vañcitā* is a variant designation for the state more usually called *vipralabdhā.*

41. Although Jayadeva does not use the term *abhisārikā,* he clearly refers to it in his use of the defining characteristic of this state, which is abandoned modesty.

42. See Dimock, *Place of the Hidden Moon,* pp. 33–35.

Gītagovinda Translation

THE FIRST PART

Joyful Krishna

"Clouds thicken the sky.
Tamāla trees darken the forest.
The night frightens him.
Rādhā, you take him home!"
They leave at Nanda's order,
Passing trees in thickets on the way,
Until secret passions of Rādhā and Mādhava
Triumph on the Jumna riverbank.   1

Jayadeva, wandering king of bards
Who sing at Padmāvatī's lotus feet,
Was obsessed in his heart
By rhythms of the goddess of speech,
And he made this lyrical poem
From tales of the passionate play
When Krishna loved Śrī.   2

Umāpatidhara is prodigal with speech,
Śaraṇa is renowned for his subtle flowing sounds,
But only Jayadeva divines the pure design of words.
Dhoyī is famed as king of poets for his musical ear,
But no one rivals master Govardhana
For poems of erotic mood and sacred truth.   3

If remembering Hari enriches your heart,
If his arts of seduction arouse you,
Listen to Jayadeva's speech
In these sweet soft lyrical songs.   4

In seas that rage as the aeon of chaos collapses,
You keep the holy Veda like a ship straight on course.
   You take form as the Fish, Krishna.
   Triumph, Hari, Lord of the World!   5

Where the world rests on your vast back,
Thick scars show the weight of bearing earth.
   You take form as the Tortoise, Krishna.
   Triumph, Hari, Lord of the World!   6

The earth clings to the tip of your tusk
Like a speck of dust caught on the crescent moon.
   You take form as the Boar, Krishna.
   Triumph, Hari, Lord of the World!   7

Nails on your soft lotus hand are wondrous claws
Tearing the gold-robed body of black bee Hiraṇyakaśipu.
   You take form as the Man-lion, Krishna.
   Triumph, Hari, Lord of the World!   8

Wondrous dwarf, when you cheat demon Bali with wide steps,
Water falls from your lotus toenails to purify creatures.
   You take form as the Dwarf, Krishna.
   Triumph, Hari, Lord of the World!   9

You wash evil from the world in a flood of warriors' blood,
And the pain of existence is eased.
   You take form as the axman Priest, Krishna.
   Triumph, Hari, Lord of the World!   ·   10

Incited by gods who guard the directions in battle,
You hurl Rāvaṇa's ten demon heads to the skies.
   You take form as the prince Rāma, Krishna.
   Triumph, Hari, Lord of the World!   11

The robe on your bright body is colored with rain clouds,
And Jumna waters roiling in fear of your plow's attack.
  You take form as the plowman Balarāma, Krishna.
  Triumph, Hari, Lord of the World!   12

Moved by deep compassion, you condemn the Vedic way
That ordains animal slaughter in rites of sacrifice.
  You take form as the enlightened Buddha, Krishna.
  Triumph, Hari, Lord of the World!   13

You raise your sword like a fiery meteor
Slashing barbarian hordes to death.
  You take form as the avenger Kalki, Krishna.
  Triumph, Hari, Lord of the World!   14

Listen to the perfect invocation of poet Jayadeva,
Joyously evoking the essence of existence!
  You take the tenfold cosmic form, Krishna.
  Triumph, Hari, Lord of the World!   15

        For upholding the Vedas,
        For supporting the earth,
        For raising the world,
        For tearing the demon asunder,
        For cheating Bali,
        For destroying the warrior class,
        For conquering Rāvaṇa,
        For wielding the plow,
        For spreading compassion,
        For routing the barbarians,
        Homage to you, Krishna,
        In your ten incarnate forms!   16

You rest on the circle of Śrī's breast,
Wearing your earrings,
Fondling wanton forest garlands.
  Triumph, God of Triumph, Hari!   17

The sun's jewel light encircles you
As you break through the bond of existence—
A wild Himalayan goose on lakes in minds of holy men.
  Triumph, God of Triumph, Hari!   18

You defeat the venomous serpent Kāliya,
Exciting your Yadu kinsmen
Like sunlight inciting lotuses to bloom.
  Triumph, God of Triumph, Hari!   19

You ride your fierce eagle Garuḍa
To battle demons Madhu and Mura and Naraka,
Leaving the other gods free to play.
  Triumph, God of Triumph, Hari!   20

Watching with long omniscient lotus-petal eyes,
You free us from bonds of existence,
Preserving life in the world's three realms.
  Triumph, God of Triumph, Hari!   21

Janaka's daughter Sītā adorns you.
You conquer demon Dūṣaṇa.
You kill ten-headed Rāvaṇa in battle.
  Triumph, God of Triumph, Hari!   22

Your beauty is fresh as rain clouds.
You hold the mountain to churn elixir from the sea.
Your eyes are night birds drinking from Śrī's moon face.
  Triumph, God of Triumph, Hari!   23

Poet Jayadeva joyously sings
This song of invocation
In an auspicious prayer.
 Triumph, God of Triumph, Hari!   24

As he rests in Śrī's embrace,
On the soft slope of her breast,
The saffroned chest of Madhu's killer
Is stained with red marks of passion
And sweat from fatigue of tumultuous loving.
May his broad chest bring you pleasure too!   25

When spring came, tender-limbed Rādhā wandered
Like a flowering creeper in the forest wilderness,
Seeking Krishna in his many haunts.
The god of love increased her ordeal,
Tormenting her with fevered thoughts,
And her friend sang to heighten the mood.   26

--•{ *The Third Song, sung with Rāga "Vasanta"* }•--

Soft sandal mountain winds caress quivering vines of clove.
Forest huts hum with droning bees and crying cuckoos.
  When spring's mood is rich, Hari roams here
  To dance with young women, friend—
  A cruel time for deserted lovers.   27

Lonely wives of travelers whine in love's mad fantasies.
Bees swarm over flowers clustered to fill mimosa branches.
  When spring's mood is rich, Hari roams here
  To dance with young women, friend—
  A cruel time for deserted lovers.   28

Tamāla trees' fresh leaves absorb strong scents of deer musk.
Flame-tree petals, shining nails of Love, tear at young hearts.
  When spring's mood is rich, Hari roams here
  To dance with young women, friend—
  A cruel time for deserted lovers.   29

Gleaming saffron flower pistils are golden scepters of Love.
Trumpet flowers like wanton bees are arrows in Love's quiver.
  When spring's mood is rich, Hari roams here
  To dance with young women, friend—
  A cruel time for deserted lovers.   30

Tender buds bloom into laughter as creatures abandon modesty.
Cactus spikes pierce the sky to wound deserted lovers.
  When spring's mood is rich, Hari roams here
  To dance with young women, friend—
  A cruel time for deserted lovers.   31

Scents of twining creepers mingle with perfumes of fresh garlands.
Intimate bonds with young things bewilder even hermit hearts.
  When spring's mood is rich, Hari roams here
  To dance with young women, friend—
  A cruel time for deserted lovers.   32

Budding mango trees tremble from the embrace of rising vines.
Brindaban forest is washed by meandering Jumna river waters.
  When spring's mood is rich, Hari roams here
  To dance with young women, friend—
  A cruel time for deserted lovers.   33

Jayadeva's song evokes the potent memory of Hari's feet,
Coloring the forest in springtime mood heightened by Love's presence.
  When spring's mood is rich, Hari roams here
  To dance with young women, friend—
  A cruel time for deserted lovers.   34

    Wind perfumes the forests with fine pollen
    Shaken loose from newly blossomed jasmine
    As it blows Love's cactus-fragrant breath
    To torture every heart it touches here.   35

    Crying sounds of cuckoos, mating on mango shoots
    Shaken as bees seek honey scents of opening buds,
    Raise fever in the ears of lonely travelers—
    Somehow they survive these days
    By tasting the mood of lovers' union
    In climaxing moments of meditation.   36

Pointing to Mura's defeater nearby
Delighting in his seductive game
Of reveling in many women's embraces,
Her friend sang to make Rādhā look back.   37

--◄{ *The Fourth Song, sung with* Rāga *"Rāmakarī"* }►--

Yellow silk and wildflower garlands lie on dark sandaloiled skin.
Jewel earrings dangling in play ornament his smiling cheeks.
  Hari revels here as the crowd of charming girls
  Revels in seducing him to play.   38

One cowherdess with heavy breasts embraces Hari lovingly
And celebrates him in a melody of love.
  Hari revels here as the crowd of charming girls
  Revels in seducing him to play.   39

Another simple girl, lured by his wanton quivering look,
Meditates intently on the lotus face of Madhu's killer.
  Hari revels here as the crowd of charming girls
  Revels in seducing him to play.   40

A girl with curving hips, bending to whisper in his ear,
Cherishes her kiss on her lover's tingling cheek.
  Hari revels here as the crowd of charming girls
  Revels in seducing him to play.   41

Eager for the art of his love on the Jumna riverbank, a girl
Pulls his silk cloth toward a thicket of reeds with her hand.
  Hari revels here as the crowd of charming girls
  Revels in seducing him to play.   42

Hari praises a girl drunk from dancing in the rite of love,
With beating palms and ringing bangles echoing his flute's low tone.
  Hari revels here as the crowd of charming girls
  Revels in seducing him to play.   43

---◆••---

He hugs one, he kisses another, he caresses another dark beauty.
He stares at one's suggestive smiles, he mimics a willful girl.
 Hari revels here as the crowd of charming girls
 Revels in seducing him to play.   44

The wondrous mystery of Krishna's sexual play in Brindaban forest
Is Jayadeva's song. Let its celebration spread Krishna's favors!
 Hari revels here as the crowd of charming girls
 Revels in seducing him to play.   45

     When he quickens all things
     To create bliss in the world,
     His soft black sinuous lotus limbs
     Begin the festival of love
     And beautiful cowherd girls wildly
     Wind him in their bodies.
     Friend, in spring young Hari plays
     Like erotic mood incarnate.   46

     Winds from sandalwood mountains
     Blow now toward Himalayan peaks,
     Longing to plunge in the snows
     After weeks of writhing
     In the hot bellies of ground snakes.
     Melodious voices of cuckoos
     Raise their joyful sound
     When they spy the buds
     On tips of smooth mango branches.   47

   "Joyful Krishna" is the first part in *Gītagovinda*

THE SECOND PART

Careless Krishna

While Hari roamed in the forest
Making love to all the women,
Rādhā's hold on him loosened,
And envy drove her away.
But anywhere she tried to retreat
In her thicket of wild vines,
Sounds of bees buzzing circles overhead
Depressed her—
She told her friend the secret.   1

--❧ *The Fifth Song, sung with Rāga "Gurjarī"* ❧--

Sweet notes from his alluring flute echo nectar from his lips.
His restless eyes glance, his head sways, earrings play at his cheeks.
   My heart recalls Hari here in his love dance,
   Playing seductively, laughing, mocking me.   2

A circle of peacock plumes caressed by moonlight crowns his hair.
A rainbow colors the fine cloth on his cloud-dark body.
   My heart recalls Hari here in his love dance,
   Playing seductively, laughing, mocking me.   3

Kissing mouths of round-hipped cowherd girls whets his lust.
Brilliant smiles flash from the ruby-red buds of his sweet lips.
   My heart recalls Hari here in his love dance,
   Playing seductively, laughing, mocking me.   4

---•◦•---

Vines of his great throbbing arms circle a thousand cowherdesses.
Jewel rays from his hands and feet and chest break the dark night.
  My heart recalls Hari here in his love dance,
  Playing seductively, laughing, mocking me.   5

His sandalpaste browmark outshines the moon in a mass of clouds.
His cruel heart is a hard door bruising circles of swelling breasts.
  My heart recalls Hari here in his love dance,
  Playing seductively, laughing, mocking me.   6

Jeweled earrings in sea-serpent form adorn his sublime cheeks.
His trailing yellow cloth is a retinue of sages, gods, and spirits.
  My heart recalls Hari here in his love dance,
  Playing seductively, laughing, mocking me.   7

Meeting me under a flowering tree, he calms my fear of dark time,
Delighting me deeply by quickly glancing looks at my heart.
  My heart recalls Hari here in his love dance,
  Playing seductively, laughing, mocking me.   8

Jayadeva's song evokes an image of Madhu's beautiful foe
Fit for worthy men who keep the memory of Hari's feet.
  My heart recalls Hari here in his love dance,
  Playing seductively, laughing, mocking me.   9

My heart values his vulgar ways,
Refuses to admit my rage,
Feels strangely elated,
And keeps denying his guilt.
When he steals away without me
To indulge his craving
For more young women,
My perverse heart
Only wants Krishna back.
What can I do?   10

---⋇ *The Sixth Song, sung with* R̄aga *"Mālava"* ⋇---

I reach the lonely forest hut where he secretly lies at night.
My trembling eyes search for him as he laughs in a mood of passion.
 Friend, bring Keśi's sublime tormentor to revel with me!
 I've gone mad waiting for his fickle love to change.   11

I shy from him when we meet; he coaxes me with flattering words.
I smile at him tenderly as he loosens the silken cloth on my hips.
 Friend, bring Keśi's sublime tormentor to revel with me!
 I've gone mad waiting for his fickle love to change.   12

I fall on the bed of tender ferns; he lies on my breasts forever.
I embrace him, kiss him; he clings to me drinking my lips.
 Friend, bring Keśi's sublime tormentor to revel with me!
 I've gone mad waiting for his fickle love to change.   13

My eyes close languidly as I feel the flesh quiver on his cheek.
My body is moist with sweat; he is shaking from the wine of lust.
 Friend, bring Keśi's sublime tormentor to revel with me!
 I've gone mad waiting for his fickle love to change.   14

I murmur like a cuckoo; he masters love's secret rite.
My hair is a tangle of wilted flowers; my breasts bear his nailmarks.
 Friend, bring Keśi's sublime tormentor to revel with me!
 I've gone mad waiting for his fickle love to change.   15

——•◆•——

Jewel anklets ring at my feet as he reaches the height of passion.
My belt falls noisily; he draws back my hair to kiss me.
    Friend, bring Keśi's sublime tormentor to revel with me!
    I've gone mad waiting for his fickle love to change.   16

I savor passion's joyful time; his lotus eyes are barely open.
My body falls like a limp vine; Madhu's foe delights in my love.
    Friend, bring Keśi's sublime tormentor to revel with me!
    I've gone mad waiting for his fickle love to change.   17

Jayadeva sings about Rādhā's fantasy of making love with Madhu's killer.
Let the story of a lonely cowherdess spread joy in his graceful play.
    Friend, bring Keśi's sublime tormentor to revel with me!
    I've gone mad waiting for his fickle love to change.   18

            The enchanting flute in his hand
            Lies fallen under coy glances;
            Sweat of love wets his cheeks;
            His bewildered face is smiling—
            When Krishna sees me watching him
            Playing in the forest
            In a crowd of village beauties,
            I feel the joy of desire.   19

            Wind from a lakeside garden
            Coaxing buds on new aśoka branches
            Into clusters of scarlet flowers
            Is only fanning the flames to burn me.
            This mountain
            Of new mango blossoms
            Humming with roving bumblebees
            Is no comfort to me now, friend.   20

    "Careless Krishna" is the second part in *Gītagovinda*

THE THIRD PART

Bewildered Krishna

Krishna, demon Kaṁsa's foe,
Feeling Rādhā bind his heart with chains
Of memories buried in other wordly lives,
Abandoned the beautiful cowherd girls.   1

As he searched for Rādhikā in vain,
Arrows of love pierced his weary mind
And Mādhava repented as he suffered
In a thicket on the Jumna riverbank.   2

--◆ *The Seventh Song, sung with Rāga "Gurjarī"* ◆--

She saw me surrounded in the crowd of women,
And went away.
I was too ashamed,
Too afraid to stop her.
  Damn me! My wanton ways
  Made her leave in anger.   3

What will she do, what will she say to me
For deserting her this long?
I have little use for wealth or people
Or my life or my home.
  Damn me! My wanton ways
  Made her leave in anger.   4

I brood on her brow curving
Over her anger-shadowed face,
Like a red lotus
Shadowed by a bee hovering above.
    Damn me! My wanton ways
    Made her leave in anger.   5

In my heart's sleepless state
I wildly enjoy her loving me.
Why do I follow her now in the woods?
Why do I cry in vain?
    Damn me! My wanton ways
    Made her leave in anger.   6

Frail Rādhā, I know jealousy
Wastes your heart.
But I can't beg your forgiveness
When I don't know where you are.
    Damn me! My wanton ways
    Made her leave in anger.   7

You haunt me,
Appearing, disappearing again.
Why do you deny me
Winding embraces you once gave me?
    Damn me! My wanton ways
    Made her leave in anger.   8

Forgive me now!
I won't do this to you again!
Give me a vision, beautiful Rādhā!
I burn with passion of love.
    Damn me! My wanton ways
    Made her leave in anger.   9

Hari's state is painted
With deep emotion by Jayadeva—
The poet from Kindubilva village,
The moon rising out of the sea.
  Damn me! My wanton ways
  Made her leave in anger.   10

Lotus stalks garland my heart,
Not a necklace of snakes!
Blue lily petals circle my neck,
Not a streak of poison!
Sandalwood powder, not ash,
Is smeared on my lovelorn body!
Love-god, don't attack, mistaking me for Śiva!
Why do you rush at me in rage?   11

Don't lift your mango-blossom arrow!
Don't aim your bow!
Our games prove your triumph, Love.
Striking weak victims is empty valor.
Rādhā's doe eyes broke my heart
With a volley of glances
Impelled by love—
Nothing can arouse me now!   12

Glancing arrows your brow's bow conceals
May cause pain in my soft mortal core.
Your heavy black sinuous braid
May perversely whip me to death.
Your luscious red berry lips, frail Rādhā,
May spread a strange delirium.
But how do breasts in perfect circles
Play havoc with my life?   13

Her joyful responses to my touch,
Trembling liquid movements of her eyes,
Fragrance from her lotus mouth,
A sweet ambiguous stream of words,
Nectar from her red berry lips—
Even when the sensuous objects are gone,
My mind holds on to her in a trance.
How does the wound of her desertion deepen?   14

Her arched brow is his bow,
Her darting glances are arrows,
Her earlobe is the bowstring—
Why are the weapons guarded
In Love's living goddess of triumph?
The world is already vanquished.   15

"Bewildered Krishna" is the third part in *Gītagovinda*

THE FOURTH PART

Tender Krishna

In a clump of reeds on the Jumna riverbank
Where Mādhava waited helplessly,
Reeling under the burden of ardent love,
Rādhikā's friend spoke to him.   1

---*⟨ The Eighth Song, sung with Rāga "Karṇāṭa" ⟩*---

She slanders sandalbalm and moonbeams—weariness confuses her.
She feels venom from nests of deadly snakes in sandal mountain winds.
  Lying dejected by your desertion, fearing Love's arrows,
  She clings to you in fantasy, Mādhava.   2

Trying to protect you from the endless fall of Love's arrows,
She shields her heart's soft mortal core with moist lotus petals.
  Lying dejected by your desertion, fearing Love's arrows,
  She clings to you in fantasy, Mādhava.   3

She covets a couch of Love's arrows to practice her seductive art.
She makes her flower bed a penance to win joy in your embrace.
  Lying dejected by your desertion, fearing Love's arrows,
  She clings to you in fantasy, Mādhava.   4

She raises her sublime lotus face, clouded and streaked with tears,
Like the moon dripping with nectar from cuts of the eclipse's teeth.
  Lying dejected by your desertion, fearing Love's arrows,
  She clings to you in fantasy, Mādhava.   5

She secretly draws you with deer musk to resemble the god of love,
Riding a sea monster, aiming mango-blossom arrows—she worships you.
 Lying dejected by your desertion, fearing Love's arrows,
 She clings to you in fantasy, Mādhava.   6

She cries out the words, "Mādhava, I fall at your feet!
When your face turns away, even moonlight scorches my body."
 Lying dejected by your desertion, fearing Love's arrows,
 She clings to you in fantasy, Mādhava.   7

She evokes you in deep meditation to reach your distant form.
She laments, laughs, collapses, cries, trembles, utters her pain.
 Lying dejected by your desertion, fearing Love's arrows,
 She clings to you in fantasy, Mādhava.   8

If your heart hopes to dance to the haunting song of Jayadeva,
Study what her friend said about Rādhā suffering Hari's desertion.
 Lying dejected by your desertion, fearing Love's arrows,
 She clings to you in fantasy, Mādhava.   9

Her house becomes a wild jungle,
Her band of loving friends a snare.
Sighs fan her burning pain
To flames that rage like forest fire.
Suffering your desertion,
She takes form as a whining doe
And turns Love into Death
Disguised as a tiger hunting prey.   10

The Ninth Song, sung in Rāga "Deśākhya"

An exquisite garland lying on her breasts
Is a burden to the frail wasted girl.
Krishna, Rādhikā suffers in your desertion.   11

Moist sandalbalm smoothed on her body
Feels like dread poison to her.
Krishna, Rādhikā suffers in your desertion.   12

The strong wind of her own sighing
Feels like the burning fire of love.
Krishna, Rādhikā suffers in your desertion.   13

Her eyes shed tears everywhere
Like dew from lotuses with broken stems.
Krishna, Rādhikā suffers in your desertion.   14

Her eyes see a couch of tender shoots,
But she imagines a ritual bed of flames.
Krishna, Rādhikā suffers in your desertion.   15

She presses her palm against her cheek,
Wan as a crescent moon in the evening.
Krishna, Rādhikā suffers in your desertion.   16

"Hari! Hari!" she chants passionately,
As if destined to die through harsh neglect.
Krishna, Rādhikā suffers in your desertion.   17

May singing Jayadeva's song
Give pleasure to the worshipper at Krishna's feet!
Krishna, Rādhikā suffers in your desertion.   18

She bristles with pain, sucks in breath,
Cries, shudders, gasps,
Broods deep, reels, stammers,
Falls, raises herself, then faints.
When fevers of passion rage so high,
A frail girl may live by your charm.
If you feel sympathy, Krishna,
Play godly healer! Or Death may take her.   19

Divine physician of her heart,
The love-sick girl can only be healed
With elixir from your body.
Free Rādhā from her torment, Krishna—
Or you are crueler
Than Indra's dread thunderbolt.   20

While her body lies sick
From smoldering fever of love,
Her heart suffers strange slow suffocation
In mirages of sandalbalm, moonlight, lotus pools.
When exhaustion forces her to meditate on you,
On the cool body of her solitary lover,
She feels secretly revived—
For a moment the feeble girl breathes life.   21

She found your neglect in love unbearable before,
Despairing if you closed your eyes even for a moment.
How will she live through this long desertion,
Watching flowers on tips of mango branches?   22

"Tender Krishna" is the fourth part in *Gītagovinda*

———◆•◆———

THE FIFTH PART

Lotus-eyed Krishna Longing for Love

"I'll stay here, you go to Rādhā!
Appease her with my words and bring her to me!"
Commanded by Madhu's foe, her friend
Went to repeat his words to Rādhā.   1

--❃{ *The Tenth Song, sung with Rāga "Deśavarādī"* }❃--

Sandalwood mountain winds blow,
Spreading passion.
Flowers bloom in profusion,
Tearing deserted lovers' hearts.
   Wildflower-garlanded Krishna
   Suffers in your desertion, friend.   2

Cool moon rays scorch him,
Threatening death.
Love's arrow falls
And he laments his weakness.
   Wildflower-garlanded Krishna
   Suffers in your desertion, friend.   3

Bees swarm, buzzing sounds of love,
Making him cover his ears.
Your neglect affects his heart,
Inflicting pain night after night.
   Wildflower-garlanded Krishna
   Suffers in your desertion, friend.   4

———•··•———

He dwells in dense forest wilds,
Rejecting his luxurious house.
He tosses on his bed of earth,
Frantically calling your name.
    Wildflower-garlanded Krishna
    Suffers in your desertion, friend.   5

Poet Jayadeva sings
To describe Krishna's desolation.
When your heart feels his strong desire,
Hari will rise to favor you.
    Wildflower-garlanded Krishna
    Suffers in your desertion, friend.   6

Mādhava still waits for you
In Love's most sacred thicket,
Where you perfected love together.
He meditates on you without sleeping,
Muttering a series of magical prayers.
He craves the rich elixir that flows
From embracing your full breasts.   7

--❈{ *The Eleventh Song, sung with Rāga "Gurjari"* }❈--

He ventures in secret to savor your passion, dressed for love's delight.
Rādhā, don't let full hips idle! Follow the lord of your heart!
  In woods on the wind-swept Jumna bank,
  Krishna waits in wildflower garlands.   8

He plays your name to call you on his sweet reed flute.
He cherishes breeze-blown pollen that touched your fragile body.
  In woods on the wind-swept Jumna bank,
  Krishna waits in wildflower garlands.   9

When a bird feather falls or a leaf stirs, he imagines your coming.
He makes the bed of love; he eyes your pathway anxiously.
  In woods on the wind-swept Jumna bank,
  Krishna waits in wildflower garlands.   10

Leave your noisy anklets! They clang like traitors in love play.
Go to the darkened thicket, friend! Hide in a cloak of night!
  In woods on the wind-swept Jumna bank,
  Krishna waits in wildflower garlands.   11

Your garlands fall on Krishna's chest like white cranes on a dark cloud.
Shining lightning over him, Rādhā, you rule in the climax of love.
  In woods on the wind-swept Jumna bank,
  Krishna waits in wildflower garlands.   12

———◆·◆———

Loosen your clothes, untie your belt, open your loins!
Rādhā, your gift of delight is like treasure in a bed of vines.
   In woods on the wind-swept Jumna bank,
   Krishna waits in wildflower garlands.   13

Hari is proud. This night is about to end now.
Speed my promise to him! Fulfill the desire of Madhu's foe!
   In woods on the wind-swept Jumna bank,
   Krishna waits in wildflower garlands. ·   14

While Jayadeva sings his enticing song to worship Hari,
Bow to Hari! He loves your favor—his heart is joyful and gentle.
   In woods on the wind-swept Jumna bank,
   Krishna waits in wildflower garlands.   15

      Sighing incessantly, he pours out his grief.
      He endlessly searches the empty directions.
      Each time he enters the forest thicket,
      Humming to himself, he gasps for breath.
      He makes your bed of love again and again,
      Staring at it in empty confusion.
      Lovely Rādhā, your lover suffers
      Passion's mental pain.   16

      Your spitefulness ebbed
      As the hot-rayed sun set.
      Krishna's mad desire
      Deepened with the darkness.
      The pitiful cry of lonely cuckoos
      Keeps echoing my plea,
      "Delay is useless, you fool—
      It is time for lovers to meet!"   17

Two lovers meeting in darkness
Embrace and kiss
And claw as desire rises
To dizzying heights of love.
When familiar voices reveal
That they ventured into the dark
To betray each other,
The mood is mixed with shame.   18

As you cast your frightened glance
On the dark path,
As you stop at every tree,
Measuring your steps slowly,
As you secretly move
With love surging through your limbs,
Krishna is watching you, Rādhā!
Let him celebrate your coming!   19

"Lotus-eyed Krishna Longing for Love" is the fifth part in *Gītagovinda*

THE SIXTH PART

Indolent Krishna

Seeing Rādhā in her retreat of vines,
Powerless to leave, impassioned too long,
Her friend described her state
While Krishna lay helpless with love.   1

--◦◄{ *The Twelfth Song, sung with* Rāga *"Nata"* }►◦--

In her loneliness she sees you everywhere
Drinking springflower honey from other lips.
  Lord Hari,
  Rādhā suffers in her retreat.   2

Rushing in her haste to meet you,
She stumbles after a few steps and falls.
  Lord Hari,
  Rādhā suffers in her retreat.   3

Weaving bracelets from supple lotus shoots
As symbols of your skillful love, she keeps alive.
  Lord Hari,
  Rādhā suffers in her retreat.   4

Staring at her ornaments' natural grace,
She fancies, "I am Krishna, Madhu's foe."
  Lord Hari,
  Rādhā suffers in her retreat.   5

"Why won't Hari come quickly to meet me?"
She incessantly asks her friend.
   Lord Hari,
   Rādhā suffers in her retreat.   6

She embraces, she kisses cloud-like forms
Of the vast dark night. "Hari has come," she says.
   Lord Hari,
   Rādhā suffers in her retreat.   7

While you idle here, modesty abandons her,
She laments, sobs as she waits to love you.
   Lord Hari,
   Rādhā suffers in her retreat.   8

May poet Jayadeva's song
Bring joy to sensitive men!
   Lord Hari,
   Rādhā suffers in her retreat.   9

   Her body bristling with longing,
   Her breath sucking in words of confusion,
   Her voice cracking in deep cold fear—
   Obsessed by intense thoughts of passion,
   Rādhā sinks in a sea of erotic mood,
   Clinging to you in her meditation, cheat!   10

   She ornaments her limbs
   When a leaf quivers or a feather falls.
   Suspecting your coming,
   She spreads out the bed
   And waits long in meditation.
   Making her bed of ornaments and fantasies,
   She evokes a hundred details of you
   In her own graceful play.
   But the frail girl will not survive
   Tonight without you.   11

"Indolent Krishna" is the sixth part in *Gītagovinda*

Cunning Krishna

As night came
The mood displayed cratered stains,
Seeming to flaunt its guilt
In betraying secret paths
Of adulterous women,
Lighting depths of Brindaban forest
With moonbeam nets—
A spot of sandalwood powder
On the face of a virgin sky.   1

While the moon rose
And Mādhava idled,
Lonely Rādhā
Cried her pain aloud
In pitiful sobbing.   2

The Thirteenth Song, sung with Rāga "Mālava"

Just when we promised to meet, Hari avoided the woods.
The flawless beauty of my youth is barren now.
　　Whom can I seek for refuge here?
　　My friend's advice deceives me.   3

I followed him at night to depths of the forest.
He pierced my heart with arrows of love.
　　Whom can I seek for refuge here?
　　My friend's advice deceives me.   4

Death is better than living in my barren body.
Why do I blankly endure love's desolating fire?
   Whom can I seek for refuge here?
   My friend's advice deceives me.   5

The sweet spring night torments my loneliness—
Some other girl now enjoys Hari's favor.
   Whom can I seek for refuge here?
   My friend's advice deceives me.   6

Every bangle and jewel I wear pains me,
Carrying the fire of Hari's desertion.
   Whom can I seek for refuge here?
   My friend's advice deceives me.   7

Even a garland strikes at the heart of my fragile body
With hard irony, like Love's graceful arrow.
   Whom can I seek for refuge here?
   My friend's advice deceives me.   8

I wait among countless forest reeds;
Madhu's killer does not recall me, even in his heart.
   Whom can I seek for refuge here?
   My friend's advice deceives me.   9

Jayadeva's speech takes refuge at Hari's feet.
Keep it in your heart like a tender girl skillful in love.
   Whom can I seek for refuge here?
   My friend's advice deceives me.   10

Has he waylaid some loving girl?
Do his friends hold him by clever tricks?
Is he roaming blindly near the dark forest?
Or does my lover's anguished mind so tangle the path
That he cannot come into this thicket of vines
And sweet swamp reeds where we promised to meet?   11

When Rādhā saw her friend come back
Without Mādhava,
Downcast and tongue-tied,
Suspicion raised a vision of some girl
Delighting Krishna,
And she told her friend.   12

--≪{ *The Fourteenth Song, sung with Rāga "Vasanta"* }≫--

She is richly arrayed in ornaments for the battle of love;
Tangles of flowers lie wilted in her loosened hair.
    Some young voluptuous beauty
    Revels with the enemy of Madhu.   13

She is visibly excited by embracing Hari;
Her necklaces tremble on full, hard breasts.
    Some young voluptuous beauty
    Revels with the enemy of Madhu.   14

Curling locks caress her moon face;
She is weary from ardently drinking his lips.
    Some young voluptuous beauty
    Revels with the enemy of Madhu.   15

Quivering earrings graze her cheeks;
Her belt sounds with her hips' rolling motion.
    Some young voluptuous beauty
    Revels with the enemy of Madhu.   16

She laughs bashfully when her lover looks at her;
The taste of passion echoes from her murmuring.
    Some young voluptuous beauty
    Revels with the enemy of Madhu.   17

Her body writhes with tingling flesh and trembling.
The ghost of Love expands inside with her sighing.
  Some young voluptuous beauty
  Revels with the enemy of Madhu.   18

Drops of sweat wet the graceful body
Fallen limp on his chest in passionate battle.
  Some young voluptuous beauty
  Revels with the enemy of Madhu.   19

May Hari's delight in Jayadeva's song
Bring an end to this dark time.
  Some young voluptuous beauty
  Revels with the enemy of Madhu.   20

The lonely moon,
Like the lotus face of Mura's foe,
Wan in love's desolation,
Is calming the surface of my mind.
But the moon is Love's friend—
It still inflicts his torments
On my heart.   21

──◄┊ *The Fifteenth Song, sung with* R̄aga *"Gurjarī"* ┊►──

Her rapt face shows the passion her lips feel kissing him;
With deer musk he draws the form of a stag on the moon.
   In woods behind a sandbank on the Jumna river,
   Mura's foe makes love in triumph now.   22

He lays an amaranth blossom in clouds of hair massed on her soft face—
A shimmer of lightning shines in the forest where Love goes hunting.
   In woods behind a sandbank on the Jumna river,
   Mura's foe makes love in triumph now.   23

He smears the domes of her swelling breasts with shining deer musk,
He makes star clusters with pearls and a moonmark with his nail.
   In woods behind a sandbank on the Jumna river,
   Mura's foe makes love in triumph now.   24

The dark sapphire bangle he slips over each lotus-petal hand
Encircles her arm's cool pale supple stalk like a swarm of bees.   Wow!
   In woods behind a sandbank on the Jumna river,
   Mura's foe makes love in triumph now.   25

Her broad hips are a temple of passion holding Love's golden throne;
He lays a girdle of gemstones there to mark the gate of triumph.
   In woods behind a sandbank on the Jumna river,
   Mura's foe makes love in triumph now.   26

He applies a shining coat of lac to feet lying on his heart
Like tender shoots tipped with pearls to honor Lakṣmī's place inside.
   In woods behind a sandbank on the Jumna river,
   Mura's foe makes love in triumph now.   27

While Balarāma's fickle brother is delighting some pretty girl,
Why does barren disgust haunt my bower of branches, tell me friend?
   In woods behind a sandbank on the Jumna river,
   Mura's foe makes love in triumph now.   28

Jayadeva, king of poets, echoes Hari's merit in the mood of his song.
Let evil dark-age rhythms cease at the feet of Madhu's foe!
   In woods behind a sandbank on the Jumna river,
   Mura's foe makes love in triumph now.   29

Friend, if the pitiless rogue won't come,
Why should it pain my messenger?
He wantonly delights in loving many women.
Why is this your fault?
See! His tenderness in love
Draws my heart to meet him.
It is trying to break away
From the pain of longing for him.   30

--⊰ *The Sixteenth Song, sung with* Rāga *"Deśākhya"* ⊱--

His eyes flirt like blue night lilies in the wind.
The bed of tender shoots won't burn her.
  Wildflower-garlanded Krishna
  Caresses her, friend.   31

His soft mouth moves like an open lotus.
Arrows of love won't wound her.
  Wildflower-garlanded Krishna
  Caresses her, friend.   32

His mellow speech is elixir of honey.
Sandal mountain winds won't scorch her.
  Wildflower-garlanded Krishna
  Caresses her, friend.   33

His hands and feet gleam like hibiscus blossoms.
Cold moon rays won't make her writhe.
  Wildflower-garlanded Krishna
  Caresses her, friend.   34

His color deepens like rain-heavy thunderheads.
Long desertion won't tear at her heart.
  Wildflower-garlanded Krishna
  Caresses her, friend.   35

His bright cloth shines gold on black touchstone.
Her servants' teasing won't make her sigh.
　Wildflower-garlanded Krishna
　Caresses her, friend.　　　　　　　　　　　　36

His tender youth touches all creatures.
She won't feel the pain of terrible pity.
　Wildflower-garlanded Krishna
　Caresses her, friend.　　　　　　　　　　　　37

Through words that Jayadeva sings
May Hari possess your heart!
　Wildflower-garlanded Krishna
　Caresses her, friend.　　　　　　　　　　　　38

Sandalwood mountain wind,
As you blow southern breezes
To spread the bliss of love,
Soothe me! End the paradox!
Lifebreath of the world,
If you bring me Mādhava
For a moment,
You may take my life!　　　　　　　　　　　　39

Friends are hostile,
Cool wind is like fire,
Moon nectar is poison,
Krishna torments me in my heart.
But even when he is cruel
I am forced to take him back.
Women with night-lily eyes feel love
In a paradox of passion-bound infinity.　　　　40

Command my torment, sandal mountain wind!
Take my lifebreath with arrows, Love!
I will not go home for refuge again!
Jumna river, sister of Death,
Why should you be kind?
Drown my limbs with waves!
Let my body's burning be quenched!   41

"Cunning Krishna" is the seventh part in *Gitagovinda*

Is she going to kill herself?

THE EIGHTH PART

Abashed Krishna

After struggling through the night,
She seemed wasted by the arrows of love.
She denounced her lover bitterly
As he bowed before her, pleading forgiveness.　　　1

--·❖{ *The Seventeenth Song, sung with* Rāga "Bhairavī" }❖·--

Bloodshot from a sleepless night of passion, listless now,
Your eyes express the mood of awakened love.
　　Damn you, Mādhava! Go! Keśava, leave me!
　　Don't plead your lies with me!
　　Go after her, Krishna!
　　She will ease your despair.　　　2

Dark from kissing her kohl-blackened eyes,
At dawn your lips match your body's color, Krishna.
　　Damn you, Mādhava! Go! Keśava, leave me!
　　Don't plead your lies with me!
　　Go after her, Krishna!
　　She will ease your despair.　　　3

Etched with scratches of sharp nails in the battle of love,
Your body tells the triumph of passion in gold writing on sapphire.
　　Damn you, Mādhava! Go! Keśava, leave me!
　　Don't plead your lies with me!
　　Go after her, Krishna!
　　She will ease your despair.　　　4

Drops of red lac from her lotus feet wet your sublime breast.
They force buds from the tree of love to bloom on your skin.
　　Damn you, Mādhava! Go! Keśava, leave me!
　　Don't plead your lies with me!
　　Go after her, Krishna!
　　She will ease your despair.　　　　　　　　　　　　　　5

The teethmark she left on your lip creates anguish in my heart.
Why does it evoke the union of your body with mine now?
　　Damn you, Mādhava! Go! Keśava, leave me!
　　Don't plead your lies with me!
　　Go after her, Krishna!
　　She will ease your despair.　　　　　　　　　　　　　　6

Dark Krishna, your heart must be baser black than your skin.
How can you deceive a faithful creature tortured by fevers of Love?
　　Damn you, Mādhava! Go! Keśava, leave me!
　　Don't plead your lies with me!
　　Go after her, Krishna!
　　She will ease your despair.　　　　　　　　　　　　　　7

Why am I shocked that you roam in the woods to consume weak girls?
The fate of Pūtanā shows your cruel childhood bent for killing women.
　　Damn you, Mādhava! Go! Keśava, leave me!
　　Don't plead your lies with me!
　　Go after her, Krishna!
　　She will ease your despair.　　　　　　　　　　　　　　8

Jayadeva sings the lament of a jealous girl deceived by passion.
Listen, sages! Heaven rarely yields such sweet elixir.
　　Damn you, Mādhava! Go! Keśava, leave me!
　　Don't plead your lies with me!
　　Go after her, Krishna!
　　She will ease your despair.　　　　　　　　　　　　　　9

The red stains her lac-painted feet
Lovingly left on your heart
Look to me like fiery passion
Exposing itself on your skin.
Cheat, the image I have of you now
Flaunting our love's break
Causes me more shame
Than sorrow. 10

"Abashed Krishna" is the eighth part in *Gītagovinda*

THE NINTH PART

Languishing Krishna

Then, when she felt wasted by love,
Broken by her passion's intensity,
Despondent, haunted by Hari's
Response to her quarreling,
Her friend spoke to her.   1

--*{ *The Eighteenth Song, sung with* Rāga *"Gurjarī"* }*--

Hari comes when spring winds, bearing honey, blow.
What greater pleasure exists in the world, friend?
   Don't turn wounded pride on Mādhava!
   He is proud too, sullen Rādhā.   2

Your swollen breasts are riper than palm fruits.
Why do you waste their rich flavor?
   Don't turn wounded pride on Mādhava!
   He is proud too, sullen Rādhā.   3

How often must I repeat the refrain?
Don't recoil when Hari longs to charm you!
   Don't turn wounded pride on Mādhava!
   He is proud too, sullen Rādhā.   4

Why do you cry in hollow despair?
Your girlfriends are laughing at you.
   Don't turn wounded pride on Mādhava!
   He is proud too, sullen Rādhā.   5

See Hari on his cool couch of moist lotuses!
Reward your eyes with this fruit!
   Don't turn wounded pride on Mādhava!
   He is proud too, sullen Rādhā.   6

Why conjure heavy despair in your heart?
Listen to me tell how he regrets betraying you.
   Don't turn wounded pride on Mādhava!
   He is proud too, sullen Rādhā.   7

Let Hari come! Let him speak sweet words!
Why condemn your heart to loneliness?
   Don't turn wounded pride on Mādhava!
   He is proud too, sullen Rādhā.   8

May Jayadeva's lilting song
Please sensitive men who hear Hari's story!
   Don't turn wounded pride on Mādhava!
   He is proud too, sullen Rādhā.   9

When he is tender you are harsh,
When he is pliant you are rigid,
When he is passionate you are hateful,
When he looks expectant you turn away,
You leave when he is loving.
Your perverseness justly
Turns your sandalbalm to poison,
Cool moon rays to heat, ice to fire,
Joys of loveplay to torments of hell.   10

"Languishing Krishna" is the ninth part in *Gītagovinda*

THE TENTH PART

Four Quickening Arms

As night came, he approached Rādhā,
Finding the force of her anger softened,
Her face weak from endless sighing.
At dusk she stared in shame at her friend's face
As Hari stammered his blissful words.   1

--*{ *The Nineteenth Song, sung with Rāga "Deśavarāḍī* }*--

If you speak, moonlight gleaming on your teeth
Dispels the dread darkness of fear.
Let your moon face lure my nightbird eyes
To taste nectar from your quivering lips!
    Rādhā, cherished love,
    Abandon your baseless pride!
    Love's fire burns my heart—
    Bring wine in your lotus mouth!   2

If you feel enraged at me, Rādhā,
Inflict arrow-wounds with your sharp nails!
Bind me in your arms! Bite me with your teeth!
Or do whatever excites your pleasure!
    Rādhā, cherished love,
    Abandon your baseless pride!
    Love's fire burns my heart—
    Bring wine in your lotus mouth!   3

You are my ornament, my life,
My jewel in the sea of existence.
Be yielding to me forever,
My heart fervently pleads!
  Rādhā, cherished love,
  Abandon your baseless pride!
  Love's fire burns my heart—
  Bring wine in your lotus mouth!   4

Frail Rādhā, even with dark lotus pupils,
Your angry eyes are like scarlet lilies.
As your arrows of love arouse emotion,
My black form responds with red passion.
  Rādhā, cherished love,
  Abandon your baseless pride!
  Love's fire burns my heart—
  Bring wine in your lotus mouth!   5

Let pearls quivering on full breasts
Move the depths of your heart!
Let a girdle ringing on round hips
Proclaim the command of Love!
  Rādhā, cherished love,
  Abandon your baseless pride!
  Love's fire burns my heart—
  Bring wine in your lotus mouth!   6

Your hibiscus-blossom foot colors my heart
As your beauty fills the stage of love.
Speak, soft voiced Rādhā! Let me dye your feet
With the rich liquid of gleaming red lac!
  Rādhā, cherished love,
  Abandon your baseless pride!
  Love's fire burns my heart—
  Bring wine in your lotus mouth!   7

Place your foot on my head—
A sublime flower destroying poison of love!
Let your foot quell the harsh sun
Burning its fiery form in me to torment Love.
  Rādhā, cherished love,
  Abandon your baseless pride!
  Love's fire burns my heart—
  Bring wine in your lotus mouth!   8

This graceful loving coaxing
Mura's foe spoke to Rādhikā
Triumphs in the joy Jayadeva sings
To delight his muse Padmāvatī.
  Rādhā, cherished love,
  Abandon your baseless pride!
  Love's fire burns my heart—
  Bring wine in your lotus mouth!   9

  Fretful Rādhā, don't suspect me!
  A rival has no place
  When your voluptuous breasts and hips
  Always occupy my heart.
  Only the ghost of Love is potent enough
  To penetrate my subtle core.
  When I start to press your heavy breasts,
  Fulfill our destined rite!   10

  Punish me, lovely fool!
  Bite me with your cruel teeth!
  Chain me with your creeper arms!
  Crush me with your hard breasts!
  Angry goddess, don't weaken with joy!
  Let Love's despised arrows
  Pierce me to sap my life's power!   11

Your useless silence tortures me, frail Rādhā.
Sing sweet lyrics in the mode of love!
Tender girl, destroy my pain with your eyes!
Beautiful Rādhā, don't be indifferent!
Don't elude me! I am deeply devoted to you.
Lovely fool, I am here as your lover.   12

Your moist lips glow
Like crimson autumn blossoms;
The skin of your cheek
Is a honey-colored flower.
Fierce Rādhā, your eyes glower
Like gleaming dark lotuses;
Your nose is a sesame flower;
Your teeth are white jasmine.
Love's flower arms conquer worlds
By worshipping your face.   13

Your eyes are lazy with wine, like Madālasā.
Your face glows like the moonlight nymph Indumatī.
Your gait pleases every creature, like Manoramā.
Your thighs are plantains in motion, like Rambhā.
Your passion is the mystic rite of Kalāvatī.
Your brows form the sensual line of Citralekhā.
Frail Rādhā, as you walk on earth,
You bear the young beauty of heavenly nymphs.   14

"Four Quickening Arms" is the tenth part in *Gītagovinda*

THE ELEVENTH PART

Blissful Krishna

Soothing Rādhā with his pleas,
Keśava dressed elaborately
And went to lie on his thicket bed.
As night fell to blind prying eyes,
Rādhā dressed in gleaming ornaments
And one woman urged her to move quickly.   1

--◆{ *The Twentieth Song, sung with Rāga "Vasanta"* }◆--

He made himself soothe you with flattery.
He made himself fall limp at your feet.
Now he waits for sensual play in his bed
On a bank of sweet swamp reeds.
    Madhu's tormentor
    Is faithful to you, fool.
    Follow him, Rādhikā!   2

Your full hips and breasts are heavy to bear.
Approach with anklets ringing!
Their sound inspires lingering feet.
Run with the gait of a wild goose!
    Madhu's tormentor
    Is faithful to you, fool.
    Follow him, Rādhikā!   3

Listen to enticing sounds of honey bees
Buzzing to bewilder tender women!
Sympathize when a flock of cuckoos
Sing Love's commands like bards.
　Madhu's tormentor
　Is faithful to you, fool.
　Follow him, Rādhikā!　　　　　　　　　4

A mass of vines with thickly clustered shoots
Quivering in the wind like a hand
Seems to be gesturing to your tapering thighs
To quicken your pace. Stop loitering here!
　Madhu's tormentor
　Is faithful to you, fool.
　Follow him, Rādhikā!　　　　　　　　　5

Strong waves of love throbbing in you
Suggest that you feel Hari's embrace.
Ask your rounded breasts if they wear
Seductive pearls or drops of pure water!
　Madhu's tormentor
　Is faithful to you, fool.
　Follow him, Rādhikā!　　　　　　　　　6

Your friends know your armed body is ready
For passionate battle, fierce Rādhā,
By the war-drum beat of your clanging girdle.
Meet his rich mood without shame!
　Madhu's tormentor
　Is faithful to you, fool.
　Follow him, Rādhikā!　　　　　　　　　7

As you cling to your friend in graceful play,
Nails on your hand are arrows of love—
Let your ringing bangles go to him!
Wake Hari! Claim his intimacy!
　Madhu's tormentor
　Is faithful to you, fool.
　Follow him, Rādhikā!　　　　　　　　　8

Jayadeva's singing devalues necklaces;
It solves the paradox of beauty.
May it always adorn the throats
Of men who devote their hearts to Hari!
　　Madhu's tormentor
　　Is faithful to you, fool.
　　Follow him, Rādhikā!　　　　　　　　9

"She will look at me, tell me a tale of love,
Feel pleasure in every limb from my embraces,
Delight in meeting me, friend," he says anxiously.
Your lover looks for you, trembles, bristles,
Rejoices, sweats, advances, falls faint
In the thicket buried in darkness.　　　　　10

Night is putting black kohl on their eyes,
Tamāla-flower clusters on their ears,
Dark lotus wreaths on their heads,
Leaf designs of musk on their breasts.
In every thicket, friend,
The night's dark cherished cloak
Embraces limbs of beautiful adultresses
Whose hearts rush to meet their lovers.　　11

As saffron-bright bodies
Of women rushing to meet lovers
Streak the night
With clusters of light,
Night spreads darkness as dense
As tamāla leaves,
Making a touchstone
To test the gold of love.　　　　　　　12

Seeing Hari light the deep thicket
With brilliant jewel necklaces, a pendant,
A golden rope belt, armlets, and wrist bands,
Rādhā modestly stopped at the entrance,
But her friend urged her on.   13

Revel in wild luxury on the sweet thicket floor!
Your laughing face begs ardently for his love.
    Rādhā, enter Mādhava's intimate world!   14

Revel in a thick bed of red petals plucked as offerings!
Strings of pearls are quivering on your rounded breasts.
    Rādhā, enter Mādhava's intimate world!   15

Revel in a bright retreat heaped with flowers!
Your tender body is flowering.
    Rādhā, enter Mādhava's intimate world!   16

Revel in the fragrant chill of gusting sandal-forest winds!
Your sensual singing captures the mood.
    Rādhā, enter Mādhava's intimate world!   17

Revel where swarming bees drunk on honey buzz soft tones!
Your emotion is rich in the mood of love.
    Rādhā, enter Mādhava's intimate world!   18

Revel where cries of flocking cuckoos sweetly sound!
Your teeth glow like seeds of ripe pomegranate.
    Rādhā, enter Mādhava's intimate world!   19

Revel in tangles of new shoots growing on creeping vines!
Your voluptuous hips have languished too long.
    Rādhā, enter Mādhava's intimate world!   20

Consecrate your joyful union with Padmāvatī!
Enemy of Mura, grant a hundred holy blessings
While poet-king Jayadeva is singing!
 Rādhā, enter Mādhava's intimate world!   21

  Bearing you in his mind so long
  Has wearied him, inflamed him with love.
  He longs to drink your sweet berry lips' nectar.
  Ornament his body with yours now!
  He worships your lotus feet—a slave bought
  With Śrī's flashing glance. Why are you afraid?   22

Her restless eyes were on Govinda
With mixed alarm and bliss
As she entered his place
To the sweet sound of ringing anklets.   23

---··❧ *The Twenty-second Song, sung with* Rāga "Varāḍī" ❧··---

All his deep-locked emotions broke when he saw Rādhā's face,
Like sea waves cresting when the full moon appears.
   She saw her passion reach the soul of Hari's mood—
   The weight of joy strained his face; Love's ghost haunted him.   24

He toyed with ropes of clear pearls lying on his chest,
Like the dark Jumna current churning shining swells of foam.
   She saw her passion reach the soul of Hari's mood—
   The weight of joy strained his face; Love's ghost haunted him.   25

The soft black curve of his body was wrapped in fine silk cloth,
Like a dark lotus root wrapped in veils of yellow pollen.
   She saw her passion reach the soul of Hari's mood—
   The weight of joy strained his face; Love's ghost haunted him.   26

Her passion rose when glances played on his seductive face,
Like an autumn pond when wagtails mate in lotus blossom hollows.
   She saw her passion reach the soul of Hari's mood—
   The weight of joy strained his face; Love's ghost haunted him.   27

Earrings caressing his lotus face caught the brilliant sunlight.
Flushed lips flashing a smile aroused the lust of passion.
   She saw her passion reach the soul of Hari's mood—
   The weight of joy strained his face; Love's ghost haunted him.   28

Flowers tangled his hair like moonbeams caught in cloudbreaks.
His sandal browmark was the moon's circle rising in darkness.
   She saw her passion reach the soul of Hari's mood—
   The weight of joy strained his face; Love's ghost haunted him.   29

His body hair bristled to the art of her sensual play.
Gleaming jewels ornamented his graceful form.
  She saw her passion reach the soul of Hari's mood—
    The weight of joy strained his face; Love's ghost haunted him.   30

Jayadeva's singing doubles the power of Krishna's adornments.
Worship Hari in your heart and consummate his favor!
  She saw her passion reach the soul of Hari's mood—
    The weight of joy strained his face; Love's ghost haunted him.   31

Her eyes transgressed their bounds—
Straining to reach beyond her ears,
They fell on him with trembling pupils.
When Rādhā's eyes met her lover,
Heavy tears of joy
Fell like streaming sweat.   32

She neared the edge of his bed,
Masking her smile by pretending to scratch
As her friends swarmed outside—
When she saw her lover's face
Graced by arrows of Love,
Even Rādhā's modesty left in shame.   33

"Blissful Krishna" is the eleventh part in *Gitagovinda*

THE TWELFTH PART

Ecstatic Krishna

When her friends had gone,
Smiles spread on Rādhā's lips
While love's deep fantasies
Struggled with her modesty.
Seeing the mood in Rādhā's heart,
Hari spoke to his love;
Her eyes were fixed
On his bed of buds and tender shoots.   1

--*{ *The Twenty-third Song, sung with Rāga "Vibhāsa"* }*--

Leave lotus footprints on my bed of tender shoots, loving Rādhā!
Let my place be ravaged by your tender feet!
   Nārāyaṇa is faithful now. Love me, Rādhikā!   2

I stroke your foot with my lotus hand—You have come far.
Set your golden anklet on my bed like the sun.
   Nārāyaṇa is faithful now. Love me, Rādhikā!   3

Consent to my love; let elixir pour from your face!
To end our separation I bare my chest of the silk that bars your breast.
   Nārāyaṇa is faithful now. Love me, Rādhikā!   4

Throbbing breasts aching for loving embrace are hard to touch.
Rest these vessels on my chest! Quench love's burning fire!
   Nārāyaṇa is faithful now. Love me, Rādhikā!   5

Offer your lips' nectar to revive a dying slave, Rādhā!
His obsessed mind and listless body burn in love's desolation.
  Nārāyaṇa is faithful now. Love me, Rādhikā!   6

Rādhā, make your jeweled girdle cords echo the tone of your voice!
Soothe the long torture my ears have suffered from cuckoo's shrill cries!
  Nārāyaṇa is faithful now. Love me, Rādhikā!   7

Your eyes are ashamed now to see me tortured by baseless anger;
Glance at me and end my passion's despair!
  Nārāyaṇa is faithful now. Love me, Rādhikā!   8

Each verse of Jayadeva's song echoes the delight of Madhu's foe.
Let emotion rise to a joyful mood of love in sensitive men!
  Nārāyaṇa is faithful now. Love me, Rādhikā!   9

            Displaying her passion
            In loveplay as the battle began,
            She launched a bold offensive
            Above him
            And triumphed over her lover.
            Her hips were still,
            Her vine-like arm was slack,
            Her chest was heaving,
            Her eyes were closed.
            Why does a mood of manly force
            Succeed for women in love?   10

Then, as he idled after passionate love,
Rādhā, wanting him to ornament her,
Freely told her lover,
Secure in her power over him.   11

Yādava hero, your hand is cooler than sandalbalm on my breast;
Paint a leaf design with deer musk here on Love's ritual vessel!
   She told the joyful Yadu hero, playing to delight her heart.   12

Lover, draw kohl glossier than a swarm of black bees on my eyes!
Your lips kissed away the lampblack bow that shoots arrows of Love.
   She told the joyful Yadu hero, playing to delight her heart.   13

My ears reflect the restless gleam of doe eyes, graceful Lord.
Hang earrings on their magic circles to form snares for love.
   She told the joyful Yadu hero, playing to delight her heart.   14

Pin back the teasing lock of hair on my smooth lotus face!
It fell before me to mime a gleaming line of black bees.
   She told the joyful Yadu hero, playing to delight her heart.   15

Make a mark with liquid deer musk on my moonlit brow!
Make a moon shadow, Krishna! The sweat drops are dried.
   She told the joyful Yadu hero, playing to delight her heart.   16

Fix flowers in shining hair loosened by loveplay, Krishna!
Make a flywhisk outshining peacock plumage to be the banner of Love.
   She told the joyful Yadu hero, playing to delight her heart.   17

My beautiful loins are a deep cavern to take the thrusts of love—
Cover them with jeweled girdles, cloths, and ornaments, Krishna!
   She told the joyful Yadu hero, playing to delight her heart.   18

— • • —

Make your heart sympathetic to Jayadeva's splendid speech!
Recalling Hari's feet is elixir against fevers of this dark time.
She told the joyful Yadu hero, playing to delight her heart.   19

"Paint a leaf on my breasts!
Put color on my cheeks!
Lay a girdle on my hips!
Twine my heavy braid with flowers!
Fix rows of bangles on my hands
And jeweled anklets on my feet!"
Her yellow-robed lover
Did what Rādhā said.   20

His musical skill, his meditation on Vishnu,
His vision of reality in the erotic mood,
His graceful play in these poems,
All show that master-poet Jayadeva's soul
Is in perfect tune with Krishna—
Let blissful men of wisdom purify the world
By singing his *Gītagovinda*.   21

Bhojadeva's heir, Rāmadevī's son, Jayadeva,
Expresses the power of poetry
In the *Gītagovinda*.
Let his poem be in the voice
Of devotees like sage Parāśara.   22

"Ecstatic Krishna" is the twelfth part in *Gītagovinda*

Studies in Oriental Culture

Translations from the Oriental Classics

Companions to Asian Studies

Introduction to Oriental Civilizations

Wm. Theodore de Bary, *Editor*